The Structural Essence Of
NATIONAL SOCIALISM

Alfred Rosenberg

INVISIBLE EMPIRE
PUBLISHING

Hard Cover ISBN: 978-1-963591-24-8

Printed in the United States of America

The German people is not marked by original sin, but by original nobility

—*Alfred Ernst Rosenberg*

CONTENTS

Alfred Ernst Rosenberg

CHAPTER

1

THE PREREQUISITES

Enigmatic and terrifying to millions appears the colossal growth of the National Socialist movement. Representatives of pre-1914 ideologies and defenders of today's dominant worldviews and political systems therefore endeavor to *"explain"* this growth of a movement once ridiculed but now rightly feared to their remaining followers—to explain it in such a way that the hypnotic influence of this new idea might be removed from their believers as much as possible. Hence, they invoke *"temporary circumstances"* like economic distress and trade stagnation, promising inevitably returning better times while also prophesying the disappearance of the National Socialist *"sickness ideology."* All these critics of National Socialism overlook that these great crises of our time are themselves signs of disease, symptoms of the most terrible kind—external parables of an internal collapse, yet also testimonies to the dominance of a spirit that sees its highest good in economic profit. And since such a spiritual-intellectual attitude runs counter to the organic structure of any communal life, the sin of a value-less generation avenges itself in political and economic catastrophes. As ultimate consequences, two possibilities then loom on the horizon of the future: that those deceived by the unscrupulous economic spirit increasingly detach themselves from the notions of loyalty, devotion, civic spirit, and integrity that still bind them, and in violent rebellion shatter a world to pieces; or that in another group the moral strength coalesces into an iron will to restore with disciplined calm the law of nature and the law of every great soul—that in the hierarchy of values, profit stands at the bottom, not at the top. Typically, in epochs of destiny both forces collide, and the struggle is then not circumvented through compromises but fought through to the ultimate decision. The outcome of this contest then often determines the further historical course of a people, a group of peoples, a class for centuries, sometimes forever.

We stand today at such a turning point of history. The spirits once unleashed by teachings that placed the absolute ego at the center of all value creation have been set free. No single overarching concept unites them; at the center of a state's legislation operate mostly persons who are agents of foreign speculative interests. There are almost no statesmen left, only syndicates of corporations, trusts, monopolies—all too often directly purchased creatures of the lowest speculative ventures. Law and judges are degraded into tools of narrowest party interests, and the last remnants of popular trust are thus undermined by the rulers of decay themselves. Inevitably so, for otherwise men who often deliver weighty speeches at world economic conferences would find themselves sitting on prison benches. This dissolution from above increasingly loosens the traditional bonds of loyalty among the masses as well, until the aforementioned day of decision arrives: chaos or resolute awakening. In the latter case, the great masses will begin their critical engagement with the immediately visible damages, some minds will delve deeper into the conditions that enabled this decay, and one or perhaps a few will give the ripe moment a new idea capable of elevating a people to greatness once more.

Thoughts come like children of God—no one can trace their origin purely empirically to its ultimate foundation. Yet the manner in which the birth of an idea is perceived reveals the characteristic mental disposition of different personalities, peoples, and masses. The widespread notion that a *"new idea"* must inevitably emerge *"fatefully"* after an *"epoch of liberalism"* is historically superficial. Indeed, history often proves otherwise, for many peoples of the greatest cultural vitality perished forever in the fires of earthly struggles without ever conceiving such a saving idea. We National Socialists do not believe that an idea has *"fatefully"* descended upon us from nebulous heights; we do not fatalistically regard ourselves as *"chosen ones,"* as the arrogant *"humility"* of many professes. What sustains us is precisely the living consciousness of organic formation from below upward, the innermost knowledge that ideas and values have risen within our breasts, driving us to powerful confession, to deeds, to sacrifices, to victories. That beautiful German saying—that it is not *"fate"* alone that is great, but the courage to bear it unbroken—reflects the same instinctive attitude, which ultimately is a question of character, the investigation of which leads to the mystery of soul-bound blood.

Those who believe they must gift us with the burden of a magical idea declare themselves fanatical opponents of purely materialistic calculation—yet through their dogma, they reintroduce it, thereby undermining the dignity of the ever-miraculous birth of an idea inhuman hearts.

Every great idea, according to Goethe, enters the world as a formative law. Every truly grand vision is always the intellectual-spiritual birth of a personality. At best, the experiences of an epoch converge through a few individuals—not by aggregation, but because they stem from the same longing, the same character, the same life-mythos.

An idea requires a body for its manifestation in this world. From this urge arose the Parthenon as well as the Sistine Chapel and the Ninth Symphony. Man, idea, and work become a spatiotemporal unity, inseparable. This fundamental insight holds true everywhere man is both subject and object, where human life is in flux, where a shifting multitude must serve as the embodiment of a thought. Here, the work is replaced by man himself.

From its earliest days, the National Socialist movement has adhered to its own law: Blood and Soil as the prerequisites for all action; personality as the grounding of a people; leadership in opposition to democratic leveling; final struggle against Marxism in its totality—that is, Social Democracy as much as Bolshevism; the replacement of incapable bourgeois elements by a new national elite...

When an idea becomes a formative, propagating force, it is indissolubly bound to its living creator. This is something anyone who has ever shaped thoughts understands instinctively, but it is also something that every Germanic character, no matter how simple, feels with immediate depth. Thus, when external enemies of organic resurgence—or those who attack the new phenomenon at its root—attempt to superficially praise the *"greatness of the idea "while dismissing names as "sound and smoke,"* it becomes clear that we are not dealing with *"idealistic"* motives or an *"idea-soul,"* but with dispositions cultivated on the asphalt of world cities—with men who comprehend neither ideas nor great personalities and are thus incapable of valuation.

As a new great will rises, many newcomers will swiftly become active without having undergone the total transformation by the idea. These join the organization in the naïve belief that the party offers a convenient platform for their schemes and ambitions—perhaps because no one else would listen to them. Such individuals often speak eagerly of *"the idea,"* imagining only the products of their own fancy and treating the new essence as an experimental object to test how far it can accommodate their previously suppressed thought-contents. For them, the personality of a true Leader is inherently vexing, because here idea and form already exist, leaving little room for posturing. Thus, with suspicious zeal, they emphasize the *"soul of the idea"* only to conclude by placing themselves in the creators' stead.

But before a doctrine—and this is eternal law—can take root as living truth, it must first be carried through the flames of time by a Leader. Those truly loyal to this idea will therefore insist on the present indivisibility of Leader and idea and must either discipline men of the aforementioned type with iron rigor or— where incurable ambition coexists with character deficiencies—expel them.

The strongest personalities and the most conscious adherents of a new great spiritual movement will refuse to degrade the painfully forged organization into a public debating club for vacillating men who mistake chatter for problem-solving. The idea stands firm, inseparably tied to the Leader; from its core emerge decisions bound to men, not bloodless abstractions, decisions that steer the world anew.

In the singular inner recognition of the idea lies true freedom; this is the inner stance of the National Socialist. Loyalty to it is loyalty to oneself. And this communal idea is strengthened by supporting the Leader in the struggle against the decay of our age—in the struggle for a great future.

This organic unity of idea, Leader, and following, permeating all levels of human potential, must be kept in mind to avoid misinterpreting the total form of the National Socialist phenomenon from the outset. And from here, the path leads into the depths of the idea itself.

Revolution in itself against decayed conditions signifies nothing. Moreover, a revolution that preaches *"absolutely new ideas"* after a people's millennia-long existence proves itself inorganic and alien to the folk. For if a people has never upheld certain thoughts or revered certain values in its history, this demonstrates that such thoughts and values do not belong to its essence. A revolution or evolution is genuine only when it serves as a means to restore a nation's disregarded eternal values—in our case, Germany's. And this is precisely the greatness of the National Socialist movement: that it is the singular German folk-idea in the forms of our time. Hence, we feel kinship with all that once made Germans proud, hence we are enemies of all that sought to falsify the Germanic essence.

We wish to act in the forms of our time. This means rejecting those often-mendacious pseudo-folkish theorists who, incapable of navigating our era—despite all its signs of decline—seek satisfaction in imitating past forms, whether in art or economics. We National Socialists affirm our epoch wholeheartedly, for we feel ourselves elements of rebirth; we know that the great ascent from 1914 to 1918 will live on in the memory of future generations as a mythical deed without parallel. We know these generations will recall witnessing a near-hopeless chaos spread across Germany's fields—until the columns of National Socialism became visible, the German nation regained its bearings under its leadership, and experienced the mightiest and profoundest rebirth. Not what others are determining our judgment, but what we ourselves embody through word, will, and deed—this is our standard for evaluating our time.

Only those who comprehend this faith and its emphatic, justified exclusivity will know how to properly situate the particulars. And only those who have experienced the struggle of blood and values in the awakening Germanic class-soul (Kassen Seele) are capable of passing judgment on our economic aims. By emphasizing character-value, the bridge is built between even the most distant epoch of the German people and the present.

CHAPTER

2

RACIAL PHILOSOPHY & STATE STRUCTURE

Every great, far-reaching intellectual movement ultimately stems from very few core ideas—often just one. This is no sign of poverty but of richness, testimony to genuine soul-formation and organic fertility, as opposed to eclecticism—the methods of those who believe they can construct something grand by stitching together many ideas. Precisely such intellectualist attempts, which arrogantly dare to criticize all else as *"lack of spirituality,"* betray the decline of creative psychic power. Nature forms an ear of grain and manifold fruit from a single seed, not by stamping together the germs of diverse plants. True forms arise in exactly this way across all spheres of life—though they demand great sacrifices whose effects then permeate every vein of other life-drives.

The violent fusion of multifarious essential traits is—in politics—democracy. Hence, in nearly all historically observable cases, it marks the political form of racial decline in a creative, strong people when it grants the same rights to alien, usually inferior groups that it had once won as the precondition for genuine world-shaping. Amid such psychic-racial decline, great minds sometimes retained insight into its nature—as when Plato, in Hellenic late antiquity, drafted a strict state based on racial foundations, likely with the subconscious awareness that the Nordic blood of the Greeks had been nearly exterminated through racial mixing and wars. For Hellas, it was too late—as it had been for India and Iran, and later for Rome. The realization that the *"eternal night"* of Böller-haas would have spread over Europe had Germanic peoples not appeared in the world is the greatest discovery of the late 19th century—one first solidified and delivered to the German people by H. S. Chamberlain, who later professed National Socialism. Later racial science and heredity theory deepened its foundations, and a vast body of literature further elaborated these insights. That all this did not remain mere paper and literature but became vital, living reality for millions of Germans today is the historic merit of Adolf Hitler and the National Socialist folk movement. Whatever the future may bring—under whatever political, economic, or social forms, interim solutions, difficulties, or struggles this movement may advance toward its goal—this historic achievement is already beyond question. All who struggled as individuals in German lands, who yearned for form amid seething chaos, who probed the depths of their own souls for the reasons behind the great collapse of 1918—they increasingly converged in a movement once ridiculed and scorned, then ostracized and persecuted, born in hopelessness in the hour of Germany's deepest humiliation within a few hearts. But this hope would surely have collapsed had it not fused with the deeply rooted faith that in a thousand German cities and villages, kindred souls envisioned similar things—that the ancient blood still coursed through those who had fought in the Great War and lived on in the descendants of the fallen.

This belief in blood's value—the primal premise of the National Socialist worldview—is no *"vulgar materialism,"* as Manchester liberals often claimed, but runs far deeper. Fundamentally, it posits that a particular creative soul, a particular character, a particular mentality is always paired with a particular racial form. It is no accident that the genius-heroic Siegfried figure is a creation and spiritual ideal of the Germanic peoples, while the swindler and inheritance-chiseler Jacob is the Jew's ideal. It is no accident that the concept of honor is the highest value in the singers of the Edda, the poet of the Hildebrand lied, the Odrun, the Nibelungenlied—reappearing in another form (the researcher's absolute truthfulness) in Leonardo, Copernicus, until its mightiest transfiguration in Faust. Conversely, it is no accident when the Jewish moral code—Talmud, Shulchan Aruch—elevates fraud against non-Jews to a guiding principle of Jewish national morality. It is no accident that the bearer of honor-thought is a slender, tall, light-eyed, vigorous man, while the descendants of Father Jacob are crooked, flat-footed, dark, curly-haired figures. It is no accident that the Pallas Athene and Apollo, with their warlike spirit, could only be depicted as the women of the Parthenon pediment and the head of Zeus show them, while the pre-Aryan spies in Homer's Thersites find embodiment just as they do on later vase paintings as backpack-carrying Oriental merchants.

From this fundamental insight unfolds the entire perspective of world history. We no longer see before us vague *"cultural spheres"* as abstract wholes; we no longer struggle to reconcile manifold forces under a single denominator or perceive harmony. Rather, the suddenly recognized struggle between different essences now appears to us as the essential truth.

Johann Jakob Bachofen, the interpreter of Greek myths, coined the term "swamp culture. "With this, he described a condition he believed he had discerned in pre-Hellenic studies. According to him, there were no firmly established states or clear societal types at that time.

People worshipped gods—mostly earth gods—and Isis was venerated in swampy thickets. From this formlessness, Hellenic form supposedly emerged, until it too relapsed—into swamp culture. Bachofen believed he had discovered a law: that every culture's end returns to its starting point. Thus, like liberalism, he asserted something mythical—that anything could emerge from anything. In reality, Greek culture did not arise from pre-Greek culture but overcame it through fierce struggle.

Nordic patriarchy triumphed over un-Nordic matriarchy; light and sky gods subjugated gods of night and earth; marriage conquered sexual collectivism; and finally, form prevailed over chaos. When Greece perished, it did not return to its origins but sank into the ethnic chaos of Asia Minor and Africa. The thin Nordic rule of the Hellenes was absorbed by the inevitable superiority of the once-subjugated peoples, and with the disappearance of Homeric character, the soul-shaped Greek man vanished forever. This struggle between different racial souls is for us today the crux of world and cultural history. Thus, the great figures of the past now pass before our mind's eye in a wholly different light, and consequently, we judge German history and the essence of contemporary intellectual and political struggles differently. We recognize no *"antiquity, Middle Ages, and modern times"*—categories that presuppose linear development where one era seamlessly follows another.

For us, new history begins wherever a new human type has prevailed over another. The essence of a German historical perspective lies in the victory of Germandom over late Rome, in the elaboration of this victory, and in the development of values bequeathed to us by Theodoric and Stilicho, the Ottonians, Frederick II, the poets of heroic lays, and the builders of cathedrals. Its standard is whether personality or outstanding deed exalted, crowned, or strengthened the Germanic soul. Thus, many strong figures from Germany's past will not vanish but gain new interpretation and significance. What once evoked love may now meet rejection; what was undervalued may stand in the brightest light of our veneration. This perspective is neither harmful nor unjust—despite countless accusations—for even our critics do not merely chronicle events and figures but evaluate them, whether from the standpoint of a dreamed-up *"humanity"* ora religio-political ideal. Above all, we consider it just to judge men—artists, thinkers, inventors, statesmen—by the consequences their deeds bore for the people from whom they sprang. Nietzsche captured this true justice best: *"Objectivity and justice have nothing in common,"* he said, defining objectivity as *"the old and contemptible neutrality of so-called scientific men."* However scrupulously truthful we may be toward genuine historical documents, we now know at last that writing history means evaluating just as shaping history for the future in the present does. For the struggle in this present is bitter denial on one side and fervent affirmation on the other—a colossal political endeavor to restore victory to the laws of aristocratic nature and the commands of Germanic blood against the bloodless, nature less world-city. Life and politics are thus not debates on green shores about *"rational expediency"* of global economic or universalist kinds, but a contest of character-values against characterlessness, of soul-formation against hostile form or formless chaos.

This very attitude finds expression in point §24 of the National Socialist program, which places Germanic moral sensibility at the center of valuation.

Article 1 of the Weimar Constitution states: *"State authority emanates from the people. "This is the liberalist formulation, which—after the "abolition" of monarchy—* shifted to preaching an intangible, nebulous *"popular sovereignty,"* declaring *"public opinion"* to be the purely mechanistic tally of votes cast secretly for a party or law. Thus, all state thinking rests on the belief that quantities guarantee quality. No valuation underlies this liberalist-Marxist thinking—though it must be added that pre-revolutionary monarchist Germany's political thought fundamentally differed little from these materialist notions. A National Socialist constitutional principle at the head of a new constitution would therefore read approximately: *"The state authority of the German Reich rests on upholding national honor!"* This would create a standard for political personalities and their actions. Though disagreements will always arise, they would at least be oriented toward a supreme value. Today there are parties whose principles outright reject the idea of national honor—even demanding the *"right"* to treason—and whose leaders promote men who, under German state authority, should long have been behind prison walls. For this reason, our entire political life is chaotic, devoid of style or aim, ever vacillating, determined by parliamentary majorities with mutually exclusive interests, only superficially papered over through occasional compromises. In the coming Reich of National Socialism, people will indeed contend over means and methods, but they must be united in their goal, or— they must be eliminated. This goal is always: the health, honor, and freedom of the German people.

Only people of kindred essence—those capable of feeling the blood and fate-bound community of all Germans as a living reality—can be united in this goal. Therefore, our program's demand that only National Comrades may hold civil rights is by no means an *"outburst of reactionary chauvinism"* but the most elementary form of self-preservation. The old state, the *"Second Reich,"* collapsed due to its neglect of this vital spirit. Germany as a spiritual, political, and racial unity will perish entirely unless a purposeful state leadership systematically removes those biologically and spiritually alien to Germanness. Adolf Hitler has repeatedly emphasized that no political or social upheaval could endure or prove beneficial unless 1. living space is expanded, and 2. the human material is biologically elevated. The unequivocal statement that Jews cannot be National Comrades thus represents the self-evident demand for a German ethnic state.

The Jew is in every respect an intermediary—through banking and stock speculation, through department stores, through dual citizenship, etc. Through these means, he has become a great financial power. But money means influence in democracy—political sway, entry into *"society."* Over time, German identity was destroyed by Jews who infiltrated intellectually and politically *"leading"* positions following the disastrous Jewish emancipation under the liberal Hardenberg. Through short-sighted marriages, old Pomeranian nobility intermingled with Jewish commercial daughters in the cities. This blood-mixing at the most sensitive point of the social body meant a paralysis of character, a degeneration of spirit, which can only be healed by removing Jews and Jewish bastards—though individual tragic cases must be accepted. Politically, this healing must be achieved by stripping them of all civil rights and subjecting them to alien legislation; racially, by invalidating marriages between Germans and Jews regardless of confession, which must inevitably have social repercussions.

In principle, though not yet pressing, the same applies to unions with Negroes and their descendants. France, which initiated Jewish emancipation, has now practically accomplished Negro emancipation. Relations between Frenchmen and Negresses—and vice versa—are scarcely remarked upon in Parisian life. Negro sculpture is fashionable; Negro sermons elevated through jazz become frequent pleasures. In recent years, a Negro even represented France in the League of Nations on colonial affairs; in 1931, this black man became Undersecretary in the Paris Colonial Office. This marks the first time in European history that a Negro has entered the government of a white state—a symbolic act with incalculable consequences. Today, the" Negro minister ruling over whites" is discussed across the colored world; the self-worth of black slave masses rises more than ever, and France now stands not only as the Republic of Rothschild but as Africa's outpost on European soil—thus the cultural peril threatening all white humanity. The same applies to Negroes and their mixed offspring as to Jews.

A favorite tactic of the Jewish press is to point out that the German people, even without Jews, are racially heterogeneous, making state-building on a racial basis impractical and only exacerbating tribal strife—from which they conclude that National Socialist racial doctrine is anti-popular and anti-state. To these typically Talmudic attempts at distortion, we counter that while racial science identifies roughly five races in Europe—each with distinct character, temperament, and mentality—German ethnicity is not a uniformly gray mixture. Unquestionably, 80% traces back to Germanic stock. This Nordic Germanic essence has shaped the vitality of German life, assimilating other European bloodlines in many cases, though undoubtedly experiencing occasional admixture. Yet all valuable individuals with partial Western or other blood will still find in the Germanic character-values their standard for action and formative element. The mysterious awakening now moving millions is precisely this self-realization of Germanic Germanness. Works of this great self-reflection proliferate beyond measure, and in many questions, 1500 years seem erased under the light of *"pre"*-history. We do not begin the history of Germanic-German essence with the year 1 but trace back millennia, drawing a straight line from the bearers of megalithic culture to Duke Widukind and Bismarck. In this great awakening, every German—wherever born—stands as a champion if he actively upholds the values of German honor and freedom. Those inferior in body and soul will naturally be excluded by these selective demands of practical action. Thus, through adherence to Germanic values, the style of future German life will emerge. Racial thought is not destructive but unifying—moreover, the ultimate bond to unite a people fractured by hardship, toil, world-cities, and Jewish poison into unity and strong statehood.

Therefore, National Socialism demands the legal removal of all African and Asian elements from German life—but equally, it has called for rallying all Germans abroad. It proposed (though rejected) that those who are German citizens must also be represented in the homeland's Reich parliament. As for Germans of foreign nationality, a disgracefully neglected duty remains: to establish an institution to represent their ethnic and cultural interests[1].

From these considerations arise the demands of §§20, 21, 23, and 25. Yet the final reflection also leads to the realm of German foreign policy.

---

1 Points 5, 7, and 8 of our program have often been misunderstood. They demanded the expulsion of those universally deemed *"troublesome aliens,"* but above all the removal of those Jewish swarms who flooded into Germany from across the world after 1914. A foreigner engaged in honest labor shall naturally face no unnecessary difficulties within Germany's means. Should Germany ever harbor non-Germans as a minority, cultural autonomy must be guaranteed.

CHAPTER

3

FOREIGN POLICY & ECONOMIC ETHICS

National Socialism's stance on foreign policy has been unequivocally consistent from the outset, remained unshaken despite all attacks, and found its most brilliant vindication in1931.

The intellectual foreign policy system of Weimar, championed by the Center Party, Democrats, and Social Democrats—though with varying nuances—rested on the following premises: they convinced the German people that the Entente's war against Germany targeted not the productive German nation itself, but the Kaiser, the princes, and the so-called *"militarists"*—a slogan particularly adopted by the Social Democrats from the enemy's propaganda and zealously perpetuated.

Furthermore, it was claimed—and Emil Barth, the Revolution's first *"People's Representative,"* reiterated in the final session of the revolutionary delegates—that the Entente would never dare to shackle Germany, since the solidarity of the international proletariat was far too immense and strong to permit exploitation of productive Germany. The same had already been written by *Forward* on October 20, 1918: *"No peace can render us defenseless."* For over a decade, the Social Democrats clung to these two dogmas in their desperate attempt to justify the 1918 revolt, for even the most obstinate among them must have wondered why they had triggered an upheaval whose consequences were unparalleled political-military impotence and unprecedented financial enslavement. Thus, they had no choice but to incessantly vilify the *"mad old system,"* thereby becoming the lackeys of enemy powers once more. Before accepting the Young Plan, the SPD's central organ, *Forward*, declared on August 30,1929, that the annual reparations were the consequences of a war against an entire world, into which the Empire had dragged us. At the Second International's Vienna congress in August 1931, Austria's leader Otto Bauer proclaimed to the cheers of Marxist delegates worldwide that the Habsburgs and Hohenzollerns had plunged the world into the catastrophe of the World War! Now the Treaty of Shame, signed by the Social Democrat Müller and Center Party leader Dr. Bell, rests—as confirmed a hundredfold—on the war-guilt lie. Upon this lie, all subsequent financial dictates are justified as rightful punishment for the German people, who allegedly bore guilt for the monstrous war. Thus, the Second International and, with it, German Social Democracy consciously became accomplices in the plundering of productive Germany.

The third thesis, championed chiefly by the Center Party alongside the Social Democrats, asserted that the central problem of European relations lay in reconciliation between Germany and France. One may view this ideal as one wishes, but it was delusional from the outset to base actual state policy on such pious hope. Examining Weimar party ideologies reveals differing rationales for the same conclusion. The Democrats and Social Democrats—as Jewish-led parties—always harbored an inextinguishable love for France, the land of Jewish emancipation. *Forward* even mid-war presented the establishment of a parliament mirroring France's as a worthy goal, and the rule of Jewish bankers in Paris via such a parliament remained a dream of Berlin's Jewish elites. For Marxist and democratic circles in Berlin and Frankfurt, *"reconciliation"* with France meant a grand banking and commercial enterprise: mergers of financial conglomerates, suppression of nationalist Germany, and tolerance of French hegemony.

The Center Party envisioned a different beloved France: France as the *"eldest daughter of the Roman Church."* During the war, despite earlier Masonic opposition, the Roman Church regained influence—Marshal Foch and other officers were devout adherents, religious orders amassed capital, and they purchased property after property on Rue Van neau. The Institute Catholique under Baudrillart operated undisturbed, and the French battle cry—"To fight France is to fight God"—was echoed by all French Catholics, joined by Belgians under Cardinal Mercier, who equated Christianity with Frenchness. This line continues unbroken today through the Archbishop of Strasbourg's stance, the display of the Tricolor in churches during ceremonies, and French bishops signing vehement nationalist appeals against Germany while insisting such appeals must not be labeled pagan. As *Germania*, the leading Center Party paper, declared, Germany must accept French hegemony as a given and logically conclude an Eastern Locarno with Poland. Should the Center's *"reconciliation with France"* succeed, Paris's military-financial dominance over Europe would be unchallengeable. Under some pretext, even the *"co-religionists in Poland"* would quietly receive stolen lands in a manner avoiding German outrage, and Germany—alongside Democrats and Social Democrats—would be relegated to third-rank status within what the Center calls the *"Occidental mission"* and the Social Democrats term *"Pan-Europe."*

Beyond ideological and racial motives, another pressure undoubtedly influenced Social Democracy. Vast sums flowed from England and France via Switzerland, Holland, and Denmark into Marxist hands in Germany during the war, and occasionally, the veil of Anglo-French *"charity"* has been lifted. The French slogan Des granges has recounted in his work *On Secret Mission with the Enemy* his experiences as a French operative in Germany. While certain self-congratulatory passages may be dismissed, the documents here produces—proving him a direct agent of French intelligence and Clemenceau—remain irrefutable. Desgranges triumphantly declares that through substantial French funding to German Social Democracy, the revolution erupted precisely on schedule. Desgranges names cautiously among his German collaborators only the late Hugo Haase. Haase, as is known, chaired the Social Democratic Reichstag faction at the war's outbreak before splitting to form the Independent Social Democratic Party with Rudolf Breitscheid, Artur Crispien, Rudolf Hilferding, and others who then relentlessly worked to deny war credits. According to this French spy's account, the leader of the Independents, the late Hugo Haase, was thus complicit in laundering French silver and gold. Naturally, this spy undoubtedly knew other gentlemen whose hollow hands received the golden stream from Paris and London. We cannot name names here but must leave it to future historians to determine which of Haase's associates were aware of this treasonous enterprise—and which profited from it while striving today to keep the SPD on its *"old course."*

From this complex of ideological and political coercion, fed by diverse sources, sprang all the slogans we associate with Locarno, the League of Nations, disarmament, Kellogg, Dawes, and Young. Repeatedly, French demands to fortify the Versailles Treaty coincided with Weimar parties' attempts to broker new *"reconciliation"* with France, portraying subsequent conference protocols as German triumphs. Today one can only grimace at the word Locarno—yet it bears remembering how years ago, Germany's Jewish and Centrist press hailed this meeting as Gustav Stresemann's monumental achievement, how global headlines echoed with *"pacification of Europe,"* and how, when Stresemann first spoke at the League, accolades proclaimed Germany now an *"equal player in world politics."* Yet amid this fanfare, the Dawes Plan—which Stresemann himself had touted as an *"economic miracle"* and *"silver lining"*—bore no fruit. Instead, as National Socialists had warned, reality struck:

Germany could not pay the demanded tributes, was incapable of continuing this endless policy of fulfillment without collapse, and urgently needed fundamental revisions to both the Versailles Treaty and the Dawes Plan.

The Paris and Hague conferences followed to amend the crumbling Dawes Pact, and again Social Democrats, bourgeois politicians, and the Center Party strained to preserve so-called *"good relations"* with France. They lacked the courage to face the true situation—to enlighten the German people about their Francophile policy's utter failure and thereby admit their own disgrace. Despite the Young Plan's ruinous terms, these parties endorsed it. In those days, the Weimar system faced for the first time a challenger destined to overthrow it completely: the National Socialist German Workers' Party. It became the voice of the plundered productive populace, fulfilling its duty by spearheading the petition and referendum against the Young Plan. Though numerically unsuccessful, this forced Young's proponents to publicly commit—through radio speeches they could never disavow—to promises we now hold against them as this submission policy collapses. It was Minister Severing who, even as Dr. Schacht refused to exceed 1.6 billion gold marks in reparations, declared that 2 billion annually would be *"relief"* worth accepting. This historic statement by Prussia's still-serving interior minister will haunt him whenever he dares appear in public. The same Severing claimed in another speech that the productive masses would *"feel"* the Young Plan's relief, and all must share in it... Foreign Minister Dr. Curtius, entrusted with continuing Stresemann's legacy, likewise asserted in a radio address that the Plan's benefits were undeniable—"no dialectic could erase this fact." His colleague Finance Minister Moldenhauer promised post-ratification would revive credit, stimulate the economy, and reduce taxes... Moldenhauer, who upon taking office vowed to fix finances in a fortnight, slunk back silently into the underworld of his German People's Party, while Democrat Dietrich carried on with Young, equally deluded by *"optimism"*—only to declare months later that hunger would scourge the nation, yet still proclaiming in 1931, amid total collapse, that Germany had experienced *"tremendous economic ascent"* since 1923!

Thus, the vaunted Young Plan took effect—yet within a year, its promised relief not only vanished but inverted. Panicked Democrats under Center Chancellor Brüning made frantic efforts to prop up the collapsing system, emergency decrees proliferated, Weimar's constitution was gutted article by article, until by late July even the Centrist *Germania* admitted these were Germany's *"darkest days,"* its people oblivious to the abyss they trod. And the first chairman of the SPD, Wels, declared—according to the *Forward* of July 10, 1931—that President Hoover's message had a *"soothing effect on anyone familiar with Germany's economic conditions at the time: 'Germany indeed stood on the brink of collapse.'"* These involuntary confessions from the black and red camps irrefutably document that after a decade of torment, the much-lauded policy of fulfillment and mutual understanding has driven Germany to the abyss.

In any other country, the government would have drawn the only possible conclusion from this catastrophic failure for the people: to resign and transfer leadership to those who for ten years had predicted every outcome with precision. At our entry into the League of Nations, the adoption of the Locarno Pact, and the Dawes Plan, we repeatedly warned that Germany would only be further shackled by these treaties, that reckoning was inevitable, that all sacrifices made to appease France would prove futile, and that years later we would face the same predicament as before—only weakened twofold or threefold. This weakening was the aim of French policy, the logical continuation of France's endeavor not merely to keep Germany militarily impotent but to cripple and ultimately annihilate it. France has pursued this goal not merely since yesterday but for a thousand years, and at every opportunity to realize it, France leads all who can be mobilized against Germany. Today it is the Poles and the Little Entente, armed to the teeth by France—which lets Briand mouth peace speeches—ready to strike should Germany, enfeebled by reparations and its Jewish press, dare resist French hegemony.

At this threshold of grave decisions, the National Socialist German Workers' Party renews its indictment: the Center Party, Social Democrats, and bourgeois democrats have weakened Germany in service to French interests, paralyzed its national will, and through hallucinatory loan policies made it a plaything of international finance. Their individual motives remain obscure to us. We confront the totality of political decisions manifest in party platforms—results now so palpable that denial is impossible. So palpable that the Center has abandoned its excuses, and Chancellor Brüning admits the winter of 1931/32may be the harshest in a century, with 7 million unemployed. This is the bankruptcy of Center, Social Democrat, and Democrat policies—a verdict we reaffirm.

How, then, has the NSDAP approached foreign policy? What clear insight did it oppose to the politics of illusion, which culminated catastrophically in Geneva's Young Plan collapse(September 1931)?

First, we emphasize that foreign policy is not merely a matter of knowledge but, above all in fateful hours, a question of character.

Momentous events in a nation's life may concentrate into mere hours. In such hours, centuries are gambled; in such moments, everything hinges on whether a people's representative possesses unyielding character.

Herein lies our conviction: what is needed is not just new ideas but an entirely new way of thinking! Yet in this transformation, we inherit a bitter legacy.

Throughout the Middle Ages, scholasticism crippled the people's common sense; later, misunderstood humanism privileged abstract thought. Time and world history were dictated by barren dogmas and lifeless theorizing. This mindset brought great domestic calamities—and even greater catastrophes in foreign policy, for while a people might still control its internal fate, the wider world beyond borders scarcely heeded its decisions.

From this abstract thinking sprang one fatal resolution after another: talk of proletarian solidarity, of global reason, culminating in dreams of Pan-Europe and eventually a positivist world republic.

These hallucinations of Germany's labor movement and academic elite shattered in August 1914—and again in late 1918—yet their lifeless ideology still finds prophets.

But abstract thought has also deeply infected the nationalist camp—our primary concern. Some assert that post-1918, the world divides into two fronts: victors and vanquished, and from this premise conclude that Germany, as the defeated, must ally with all oppressed peoples. This is a perilous fallacy.

In truth, the Entente's 1914 fronts arose not from organic necessity—Clemenceau and Lloyd George admit in their memoirs how fragile this alliance remained even in 1917, how hastily its cracks were papered over, how only shared fear of Germany held it together.

Nor did the victors' front endure organically thereafter, but due to the incompetence of German foreign policy, which failed to exploit existing fissures and loosen this brittle coalition.

We reproach our past foreign policy not for sacrificing aims piecemeal, but for sacrificing the wrong points for ten years—creating no breathing space to regroup our strength, only further exhausting the nation, as every concession whetted the insatiable enemy's appetite.

Bismarck's policy was consistently aimed at isolating France. Yet this fundamental axiom of German statesmanship had been forgotten. France never recovered from its 1871 defeat. Immediately, it sought allies against Germany.

Already then, it turned swiftly toward Russia. But Bismarck, through the Reinsurance Treaty, managed to wrest Russia largely from France's grasp. He secured Russian influence in the Balkans—even going so far as to contemplate opening the Dardanelles against England if necessary. In return, Russia promised neutrality in case of war with France. Before concluding this treaty, Bismarck had sounded out England. But Britain, confident in its isolationist policy, refused in its sense of power and might. Later, when Britain approached Germany, the treaty was already signed, leaving no room for accommodation.

Today our newspapers repeatedly claim that Germans and French are spiritually so akin that a *"European reconciliation"* would be possible if only the two nations reached understanding. Such literary wordplay cannot guide foreign policy.

Against our current foreign policy—teetering on collapse—stand the iron facts of a millennium of history, France's relentless thrust lines that no newspaper rhetoric or academic chatter can withstand. From its inception, France has obeyed a very specific political dynamic law. When Louis XI, the true architect of France's centralized state, had subdued his barons and counts, he declared: France's next objectives were Alsace, Lorraine, and the Rhine's left bank. Every subsequent ruler, whether monarch or republican, pursued this goal. Even the 1870/71 war was instigated by Napoleon III solely to achieve it.

This is an immutable reality, unaltered by the talk of certain circles in Paris and Berlin. Germany once faced a decisive moment. Had it recognized this truth, it might have altered its destiny during the 1904/05 Russo-Japanese War, when Russia's forces were diverted eastward—freeing Germany from its eastern nightmare. At that time, fearing reckoning over Morocco violations (France had broken its Morocco agreements without consulting Germany), Paris trembled at the prospect of war. The memoirs of Germany's London ambassador, Freiherr von Eckardstein, reveal details of these fateful days that passed unnoticed; this ambassador, moving only in Jewish high-finance circles, collaborated with the French premier to suppress any militant response in Germany[1].

For Chancellor, von Bülow and his circle, serving world peace took precedence over seeing Germany strong and consolidated! Those were moments demanding character—and character was absent! Chief of Staff Schlieffen later stated: had conflict arisen then, we would have crushed France.

To understand France's postwar position, one must see it as a python digesting a calf—gorged on conquest, it needed rest. Rest to refortify its German frontier from the North Sea to the Alps; funds to rebuild its devastated north; rest to arm its new allies. For make no mistake: after 1918, France never abandoned its centuries-old Rhine obsession.

France's ambition extends beyond the Rhine—it seeks Germany's annihilation. Germany must be erased as a European power!

To this end, all means are justified: political, military, financial. In each domain, French policy displays uncanny agility and skill.

Here we confront the terrible fact: having ended one war, France immediately began another—waged by other means. — — — Germany pays, and pays—financing France's rearmament, its eastern fortifications, even its navy. Germany's reparations dredge French harbors, while its toil arms its mortal foe!

For twelve years, Hitler has proclaimed this truth. The entire National Socialist movement maintains unshakably: no true understanding is possible if *"understanding"* implies equality between peoples. France will never voluntarily concede this.

We do not claim to prepare revenge against France. On the contrary, we've declared that had France shown reason, it would have unshackled Germany's

---

1 For further details and the full exposition of NSDAP foreign policy, see Hitler's *Mein Kampf* (WDR 7.20) and my work *The Future Path of German Foreign Policy* (both published by Frz. Eher Nachf., Munich).

eastern expansion rather than blockaded it. We seek not France's destruction, but a German state no longer prey to French ambitions! We preach no war against France—we demand living space for a great cultural nation, land for eastern farmers to feed our people.

Today these great issues confront us anew. In the east, across lands won and cultivated by German blood, our mortal enemy spreads—Poland, France's satellite! To deny this is to renounce a thousand years of German history, sacrifice, and struggle.

Freeing Germany's eastern farmers is the foundation of our national rebirth!

Therefore, the current task of German foreign policy—today more than ever—is to determine which states have no interest in this French hegemony over Europe and its satellites, as endorsed by the Centre Party.

Italy needs living space to expand; to prevent losing its surplus population to South America, it seeks territories with islands to incorporate into the homeland. Italy was lured into the war with grand promises—a slice of Asia Minor, Greek islands—all of which were later revoked. Moreover, Italy has interests in the Balkans, where it seeks to break from the victors' front, contrary to French designs there. Our foreign policy failed to exploit this. Yet now, after twelve years of slandering and opposing Fascism, Chancellor Brüning had to travel to Rome— not voluntarily, but because he witnessed the complete collapse of the Centre Party's foreign policy ideology.

In June, Reichsbank President Luther declared: after fourteen years, the budget is balanced again. He traveled to London, Paris, and Basel, only to return, bitterly disappointed. He encountered conditions that, as Reichsbank president, he could not accept.

The French government did not officially present these demands, but newspapers published them on behalf of the French ministry, enabling the Jewish press in Berlin to claim France had made no official conditions. Ultimately, Paris dealt Germany a devastating blow in the matter of the customs union.

In August 1931, to the world's astonishment, Hungary abandoned its system, which had closely tied its fate to Germany's. Hungary had pursued this policy with absolute loyalty. Yet today, it has been forced to grovel before its bitterest enemies because Germany showed no sympathy for *"Horthy's Hungary."*

France now strives to shield its Polish kin in the East as well, having long engaged in negotiations with Moscow. No one can predict the outcome of these plans. But their aim is clear: to render Poland independent and poised to strike at East Prussia.

England has endured numerous internal struggles and currently faces its gravest divisions in a decade. Yet the threat posed by France's air fleet has awakened British instincts to expand their own. The additional challenge from French financial power will, one hopes, prompt further defensive measures.

In foreign policy, Germany confronts these realities just as it did ten years ago—sacrifices are made endlessly, yet all are futile because they only enrich France. When the advocates of the Policy of Fulfillment claim no other foreign policy is possible with this people, we respond: of course no foreign policy can be conducted with Marxism, for Marxism is inextricably linked to our mortal enemy. Yet it was precisely this so-called bourgeoisie that, contrary to National Socialist principles, pursued French-aligned policies with this very Marxism, attempting to suppress the nation's awakening through this French-inspired, anti-popular Marxism. Until no national segment of the people stood behind the Policy of Fulfillment any longer.

The specific questions and solutions that will arise for the future state are not the subject of this examination; they belong to later insights, contingent circumstances, and prevailing possibilities. What matters is the fundamental realization that everything depends on preventing the French system from dominating all of Europe. Here, our opponents tell us that with a National Socialist government in power, the moment may soon come when France marches into Germany.

That France can invade if Germany's dynastic power grows further is self-evident. And this power will only increase precisely because of the past and present Policy of Fulfillment.

But France will think twice before taking such a step if it faces a spiritually fortified Germany—one that does not stand alone but is aligned with all of France's adversaries in a united front. This raises the risk of a French incursion by 80 percent.

From this complex, it follows that even foreign policy rebirth must begin with a rebirth of character: an iron will that recognizes France clearly and soberly, then marshals all forces to secure the life of the German people.

More cannot be elaborated here. What remains essential is the foundational insight into assessing the French problem, from which the correct perspective for judging all other foreign policy questions also emerges.

Since this work is not an economic policy treatise, I will confine myself to fundamentals—establishing the standpoint from which the National Socialist approaches economic questions as well.

G. Feder rightly emphasized, in contrast to the purely private, individualistic notion of profitability, that in our view, the economy must fundamentally serve to meet needs. Thus, the principle *"The common good before the private good"* should be interpreted to mean that national necessity takes precedence over all private profits. This happily outlines the task of a national economy. But we must delve deeper still.

If we initially establish that racial health and hereditary fitness are the very prerequisites for the state (and culture), and that politics is therefore a means in service of preserving blood, then the same task applies to the economy. The goal of all economic activity must be to strengthen the people in their struggle for existence, in their conflict with external powers and internal destructive forces. Thereby, the economy assumes a biological mission, and only once this primary task is recognized and acknowledged can the evaluation of various economic systems begin. We thus firmly reject any dogmatism of form—and herein lies the primary distinction between National Socialism and purely theoretical minds and abstract speculations that now sprout like mushrooms in the wake of the collapse of purely private-capitalist doctrines. Even in nationalist Germany, there are enough dreamers and literati who now pass for particularly *"revolutionary"* and wish to nationalize or socialize nearly everything. But we believe that the true state must restore the valuation of genuine personality not only in politics but also in the economy. For, strange as it may sound, it is precisely this that has been increasingly suppressed under the rule of the liberalist system. Today, financial capital—the anonymous corporation—rules over the inventor and creator. To liberate the genuine personality in technology and economy, it must be freed from the speculative self-interest of profiteering foreign racial elements. Therefore, National Socialism demands, for the protection of the true national economy, the nationalization or state control of major banks and large-scale credit institutions, as well as the abolition of anonymous corporations. German industry is already far too powerless to free itself from the clutches of mostly Jewish big bankers—only a strong political movement can accomplish this. And National Socialism has undertaken this mission not out of love for industry and commerce, as certain *"revolutionaries"* deceitfully claim, but in the recognition that this is the only way to assist the German working class as well. For if health and strength of the nation are the highest good for a racial state—and simultaneously the strongest economic capital—and if credit control rests in the hands of National Socialist statesmen, only then can direct influence over the fate of millions of workers be achieved. If today the industrialist and other entrepreneurs are manipulated by financial-capitalist private interests, they will be replaced by the common good, represented by the state government, which will then have the authority to remind the entrepreneur emphatically of his duty to the people as a whole.

Many generations of German workers have been cheated of their birthright to life by the onslaught of technology, Their great protest against this was thus deeply justified, and the struggle against the immediately visible *"smokestack barons"* was understandable—in many individual cases, even necessary. The liberalist state, the *"Second Reich,"* proved incapable of solving the great problem placed before it; it sought only to master it *"from above"* (Bismarck) or approached the questions with *"charity"* and palliatives. That this concerned enforcing Germanic conceptions of justice against a bastardized rural world was grasped by only a few of the intellectual leadership (Verrot, Lagarde, Niecks).

This consideration already leads us away from disputes on the rational level (whether this or that form is expedient)—we descend with it deep into the realm of volitional forces, of values. For the uprising of the Fourth Estate was originally a protest born of a sense of justice, and the National Socialist movement is essentially the redirection of this instinct, which had strayed into Marxism, back into the realm of these character values. The guilds of the Germanic Middle Ages were required to be as pure as if they had been read from the scriptures; under ancient Germanic law, only a man of honor was legally competent—the bankruptcy of a Hanseatic merchant was the most terrible fate that could befall him. Today, Social Democracy protects the greatest swindlers (Barmat, Sklarek, etc.) and thereby demonstrate that it must be inherently incapable of fighting the corrupt capitalist world—indeed, that it is merely an appendage of the worst dregs of that world. Bankruptcy today—in many cases certainly culpable—has become a welcome means of *"business liquidation "for scoundrels, with little serious objection taken. From this starting point, in the restoration of a Germanic economic ethic, the healing of our life must proceed. If the idea of honor is proclaimed the highest good of the people, if the entire economic behavior of the state, communities, and individuals is measured by the concept of honor, and if the judge delivers his verdict from this standpoint—only then are the first and most necessary conditions for the much-discussed "economic recovery"* met. And from this realm of values, the forms, the technical necessities in individual questions, will then emerge. Here, too, accompanied by the further insight that it is the overall political fate of the nation that causes an economy to flourish or perish.

After 1871, we did not solve the problems—we had the choice, to follow in the footsteps of Henry the Lion and Frederick the Great further eastward or to over-industrialize. We chose the second path, the path of *"economic"* conquest, and instead of creating a single enemy as in the first case (Austria), we earned the hostility of all nations already engaged in world trade—without even drawing the logical conclusion of an alliance with Austria at the sacrifice of Austria-Hungary. Today, this reckless policy is continued under the pressure of the tribute policy, filling France's coffers and provoking resistance from all other states as well. Until a decisive reversal is effected here, no serious talk of economic recovery is possible.

Foreign and domestic policy thus form an organic whole. Without a rebirth of character and a cleansing of inner life, no unified and forceful foreign policy is possible—and without a bold, essentialist foreign policy, it will be all the more difficult to truly accomplish the comprehensive healing of the nation.

In this context, one question has increasingly come to the forefront amid the economic-political struggles of our movement: agricultural policy. What is unfolding today under the influence of the biologically trained National Socialism is the restoration of the prestige of our peasantry. Mocked in the Middle Ages by the ruling class, later cheated of his Germanic rights by Roman-law jurists, crushed by

Latin-speaking judges; derided in liberalist times as intellectually backward and stupidly stubborn; threatened by Marxism with open extermination—today, the German peasant celebrates his day of honor through the NSDAP. We, who have freed ourselves from alien legal concepts and the liberalist-Marxist underworld, recognize the peasant not as one estate among estates but as the prerequisite of our economic existence—indeed, as the primal source of our racial renewal altogether. (W. Darré.) We see generations in the metropolis perish swiftly, see the first-born dying on asphalt—and from a protest against these manifestations of decline, we turn back to our village. Not in the sense of pseudo-Romantic sentimentality, but from the deepest awareness that in the preservation of the peasant ethos—in its purity, industriousness, and fertility—lies also the hope of a coming rebirth.

To the peasants, we National Socialists can proudly say: it was not your narrow-minded old estate parties that made your salvation possible, but soldiers, tradesmen, even poor industrial workers who fought and bled for you as well. What the World War, what Marxism committed as crimes against the peasant, National Socialism has now made good—and ever greater numbers of peasants now understand that they, too, must place the totality of the nation above all else and thus fight in Hitler's German freedom movement, which in so many ways is the modern continuation of the brutally suppressed peasant uprisings of the 16th century.

Only when state credit lies in the hands of a National Socialist government will *"profitable"* luxury and export industries not be artificially inflated while peasant lands are auctioned off—instead, every productive enterprise will receive the necessary support. Precisely for national economic reasons as well: for even if export profits may appear large, within the broader framework they represent a loss when ancient farm steads must be sold because of them, as is already the case a thousandfold today. Yet another proof that we possess no national economic mindset whatsoever, only various class-profiteering group interests.

Thus, the problem of an economic rebirth also integrates into the restoration of the foundation of values in societal life, into foreign policy freedom and territorial expansion, into the strengthening of the agricultural estate as the prerequisite for our people's very existence. Once this is achieved, we can confidently leave the solution of individual questions to those who have fought for our political freedom[2].

---

2 Individual economic questions are discussed in detail by the Economic Department of the Reich Leadership of the NSDAP.

CHAPTER

4

WORLDVIEW, RELIGION, POLITICS

The chapter on National Socialism and religion has continuously occupied minds since the emergence of the NSDAP. Adolf Hitler took from the outset the statesman's position,regarding the fact of differing religious affiliations as given and insisting that the political movement remain elevated above religious conflicts. In his work *Mein Kampf*, he emphasizes—from the ancient Germanic sensibility (which had guided the Visigoths and Theodoric as much as the *"pagan"* Frisian kings)—respect for every genuine religious conviction. He also saw in Christianity, broadly understood as a phenomenon bound to Jesus Christ, an actual, existing spiritual foundation of our being, and from this comprehensive attitude of his and the other founders of the National Socialist movement arose the much-disputed §24 of the Party Program. One would think every Christian denomination should have welcomed the rise of a workers' movement that energetically set itself against the soul-killing, atheistic Marxism, that further championed idealistic thought against the Mammon-worship of our age, and that—like Jesus once did—wielded the whip against the money-changers and merchants. But the opposite occurred! Precisely that party which claimed to practice only Christian politics rose to fight National Socialism and, the stronger it grew, aligned itself ever more with the Social Democrats hostile to all religion. It formed coalitions to exterminate the Christian-German workers' movement and supported those forces that for years had financed the church-exit movement and continued this propaganda even after coalition agreements, up to the present day.

There was something the Marxists hated as much as the Centre Party did: the conscious racial sensibility and appeal to Germanic moral feeling, as expressed in §24. At Catholic Congresses—which were effectively Centre Party rallies (Constance 1923)—German nationalism was denounced as *"the greatest heresy,"* and bishops (Mainz) and cardinals (such as Bertram) competed in condemning this *"neo-paganism,"* forbade membership in the NSDAP as church princes, even excluded Catholic National Socialists in some places from the sacraments. They invoked Catholic doctrine. The remarkable fact amid these attempts is that in strictly Catholic Italy, the most extreme nationalism has become state policy, and that the Pope—who for decades had rejected any reconciliation with liberalism—made peace precisely with the leader of this most fervent nationalism, even calling Mussolini after the Lateran Treaty a *"man of Providence."* From Italian church organs now resounds more frequently the royal anthem, and among cardinals of Italian origin runs the whispered remark that beneath their purple, they all wear the black shirt of Fascism.

The German people demand nothing more than that they, as a whole, be granted the same right to national pride—the right to establish a genuine national state based on their character. If their church princes deny them this in the face of the indisputable Italian precedent, on grounds of *"Catholic doctrine,"* then only two conclusions remain: either there are two Catholic doctrines, or the faithful masses are being deliberately misled to achieve political ends. Since the first case is impossible (the Roman Church has only one doctrine), the second must be true. The Centre Party may field Zionists and representatives of Southern cultural associations as Reichstag candidates, may even admit Protestants a spowerless members, but it remains a strictly Catholic confessional party. Just as Marxism seeks to externalize the nation's division through the doctrine of class struggle, so the Centre has declared confessional class war on the German nation, dragging spiritual and religious strife into the sphere of petty politics— and just as the Social Democrat sees only his class,so the Centre leader sees only his confessional interest. This party thrives on conflict,which is why it has hated the NSDAP from the first day with all its heart, because the latter exemplified religious tolerance within a party as a living model. Religious disagreements and philosophical debates had to be conducted outside the party organization; the moment they assembled, the moment the SA donned their brown shirts, there were no more Catholics and Protestants—only Germans fighting for their homeland and their people's honor. No comrade in the NSDAP is asked whether he is Catholic or Protestant, whether he belongs to the German Church or is a Reformist; what matters is his service to German freedom. The deep wounds of the Thirty Years' War finally began to close in the National Socialist movement, just as the wounds of Marxist and bourgeois class struggle began to heal. Then rose the concentric assault of all those political upstarts who had sucked their parasitic existence from these wounds in the national body. The Marxists shrieked"Capitalist scum!", the bourgeois leaders screeched *"National Bolsheviks!"*, the Centre cried *"Enemies of all religion!"* They all lied.

Never has religious feeling been treated with such unscrupulousness as by the Centre Party and the political prelates who lead it. And one point in particular was repeatedly targeted by these zealous dialecticians.

National Socialism claims, as stated earlier, to be not merely an ordinary political party but also a worldview. To strengthen its fight against German nationalism, the Centre Party points to this worldview and declares it *"pagan, anti-Catholic racial corruption."* Regarding this battle cry—now more lifeless than ever—it must be said that racial science established the diversity and differing value of races, just as any discovery in the physical or chemical realm would. Such a discovery cannot be combated by dogmas or condemnations, and the Church has repeatedly had to bow to these facts. When Copernicus first advanced his heliocentric theory—when the flat earth with heaven above and hell below suddenly became a sphere floating freely in space—an entire world of dogmas rose against this doctrine. Until 1827 (!), all works teaching this solar system remained on the Index. Copernicus's discovery naturally demanded an entirely different worldview than the biblical one, a different way of perceiving the world, yet it did no harm to genuine religion, which springs from the human soul. And it took 300 years for both the Roman and Protestant churches (which had also branded Copernicus a fraud and deceiver) to accommodate this new worldview— yet in the end, they had to submit to it.

Another example is the treatment of the mother tongue. Only the use of pagan (here the term is entirely justified) Latin was permitted; Meister Eckhart was fiercely attacked for favoring the German language, while the entire German people owes to Luther its unifying High German language—something shared by Protestant and Catholic alike, even if the Jesuit Bettler calls Luther a *"nun-defiler,"* a *"filthy sow,"* or a *"swine's snout."* The decrees of the Jesuit order once stated that the mother tongue should never be permitted in all school matters. By 1830, the order was forced to at least permit the mother tongue for poetry—at a time when Goethe was completing his life's work! And the well-known Jesuit Father Duhr admitted: *"This remained the rule henceforth: Practice in the mother tongue is commendable, but it shall not be made a separate school subject."* This persecution of a people's most precious possession was overcome; today, the Roman Church itself often advocates for the mother tongue while safeguarding its believers' interests.

The situation is quite similar regarding racial science in relation to religion. A bishop's,cardinal's, or even the Pope's judgment on race is in this case purely a private opinion on a biological—or politically derived—issue that lies outside the purely religious authority granted by faithful Catholics. A dogmatic pronouncement can no more undo a scientific discovery than it could reverse Copernicus's findings.

In the Middle Ages, researchers were burned as sorcerers; today, the Vatican builds its own radio station, which a Torquemada would surely have cursed as the devil's worst handiwork. Therefore, the fight against racial science is not religious in nature but a battle waged by political interests that had previously rallied their voters on other grounds. An anathema against blood consciousness will thus be overcome for the same reason Copernicus prevailed—though it is a historical irony that one of the most sensitive researchers of heredity laws was a Catholic priest: Gregor Mendel...

From these observations, it follows that worldview and religion are not the same. A worldview can exist outside religion (atomistic cosmology, naturalistic monism), but it can also encompass religion. The National Socialist movement is a people's politics based on a new yet ancient and firmly grounded worldview of blood value. It seeks to protect healthy, good blood—whether one calls this God's creation or ironclad natural law—and in both cases, National Socialism offers a constructive principle,which in itself signifies a religious foundation. The most delicate spiritual questions about God and immortality, fate and grace, the political militant movement leaves to the individual for decision. They may seek those pastors and spiritual guides they require to cultivate their innermost life.

The opponents of consciously German identity in Bavaria, Silesia, and the Rhineland, in their hatred, go so far in their critique of §24 of the National Socialist Program as to claim there is no such thing as a distinct *"Germanic moral sensibility"* that could serve as a standard for action. This amounts to a deliberate denial of German cultural consciousness altogether, a terrible disrespect for the value of their own ancestors. For without the character traits prerequisite to state and societal formation, Germany as a living entity would never have emerged; without strength and will to shape, the very land would not have been conquered—land on which now sit chiefly those who revile these pioneering forebears while being utterly estranged from the founders of prosperity, freedom, and statehood. Closer examination reveals them as parasites on their fathers' achievements. And if state-building character was already part of Germanic morality, this morality revealed itself so grandly in other aspects of life and art that it takes unparalleled audacity to equate Germanic essence with that of Hottentots or Jews. When, for instance, the Vandal Stilicho became regent of Rome, one of his first acts was to ban gladiatorial combat—that terrible symbol of a degenerate, brutalized world that had adopted these cruel games from Near Eastern despots. The great Ostrogoth Theodoric later did the same, replacing gladiatorial slaughter with knightly tournaments. Without falling into one-sided glorification of Germanness, one may still say that, for example, the *Sigrdrífumál*—the exalted song of a proud woman—reflects a profound spiritual beauty, as does the noble, magnanimous figure of Siegfried; and even in Hagen, something absolute shines through—his loyalty to his king.

Germanic morality was that deep truthfulness toward oneself, that desire to account for one's own being, nature, and the cosmos. From this longing sprang the mystics, the great explorers of nature, up to Immanuel Kant's sublime doctrine of duty. And in German music, this soul became world-transcending life—so that the denial of this Germanic-German value constitutes an assault aimed at destroying the German soul, which has shaped the world since time immemorial. That such a denial could be openly expressed demonstrates the profound decline Germany as a people is suffering today, but also reveals the necessity of a united popular resistance—regardless of religious affiliation—against actions whose ultimate consequence is racial chaos and the physical, then political, demise of the German nation.

The reference to *"Germanic moral sensibility"* is directed against the so-called Talmudic religion. However one may evaluate the Old Testament—whether as purely Jewish degradation or as the adulteration of other, even Aryan, ideas—may be left to the research of individual scholars. The NSDAP imposes no restrictions on such inquiries but, as a party, takes no position on them. This may serve to enlighten particularly orthodox Protestant circles, which have directed their attacks against the NSDAP from this angle. There can be no doubt, however, about the stance toward the later development of Jewish character in the Talmud and the Shulchan Aruch. It is unequivocally clear that we are dealing here with a *"morality"* that shamelessly aims to defraud non-Jews and, through this so-called *"religious"* yet falsely labeled ethical code, to mold the entirety of Jewry into a uniformly acting community. Jewish representatives have attempted to dismiss certain passages as *"forgeries,"* but even if one were to disregard the disputed sections, more than enough remains to categorically reject this immorality both from the standpoint of Christian doctrine and Germanic moral sensibility.

This includes the hotly contested issue of ritual slaughter. According to the unanimous opinion of all German experts, shechita constitutes an appalling act of animal cruelty. Countless petitions from humane veterinarians and German associations have repeatedly documented the brutality of this Jewish ritual, and the NSDAP immediately took up the fight to abolish this torture. This attitude toward animals as fellow living beings on this earth is also part of the now-slandered Germanic moral sensibility, which one does not find among parasitic peoples. Schopenhauer and Wagner spoke profoundly and emphatically on behalf of creatures, and the NSDAP professes this worldview. One might expect the Centre Party and Bavarian People's Party to stand united in this cause, since Christian ethics also oppose all unnecessary suffering.

Yet the BVP consistently voted against banning ritual animal cruelty in the Bavarian parliament—a ban that ultimately passed only with Social Democratic support. This was justified with"religious tolerance," thereby declaring blatant animal cruelty a—religion.

The Centre Party[1] adopts the same stance in the Reich, a concentration of anti-Christian and anti-German sentiment, motivated by fear of the Jewish moneybag's power.

For National Socialism, the Talmud's stance on the person of Jesus Christ is the final and decisive factor. Many religious forms trace back to Him; mutually exclusive dogmatic structures claim Him as their foundation. The NSDAP does not involve itself in these theological battles, as they lie outside its purview. Yet it regards the towering personality of Christianity's founder with profound reverence. It has always upheld His name and combated every mockery—which cannot be said of the Centre Party or BVP. The Talmud addresses Jesus in several passages, in unspeakably defamatory terms. He is called *"the Hanged One," "the Bastard," "Son of a Whore."* The enduring hatred is especially evident in the Talmud's depiction of Jesus being punished in hell *"with boiling excrement"* for His deeds. The Talmud remains the binding moral code for the overwhelming majority of Jews today—yet this did not deter the Centre Party from reinforcing its anti-Christian practice by daring to present Georg Kareski, chairman of Berlin's Jewish community, as its Reichstag candidate in 1930!

Kareski is furthermore an Eastern Jewish immigrant, thus particularly Talmud-loyal, and a Zionist leader—that is, a representative of extreme Jewish racial nationalism. While the Centre venomously attacks German nationalism as heresy, it acknowledges pan-Judaism by incorporating its extremists into the party leadership. As a final—damning—detail, Kareski is a director under the Jewish currency speculator Jakob Michael...

No greater mockery of Jesus Christ than the candidacy of the Talmudic Jew Kareski can be imagined. It strips the Centre Party of any remaining right to present itself as representative of Catholic—or indeed any—Christian thought. The facts speak for themselves; no hypocritical lip service can obscure them.

---

1 *"The Centre Party knows no Germanic moral sensibility,"* stated the party's official bulletin (No. 12, 1930). Nor did anyone expect otherwise.

Years ago, when a Munich exhibition displayed a crucifixion piece that grotesquely mocked Christ, Adolf Hitler protested this affront to Christian Germany—which the Bavarian People's Party government had tolerated. Only then was the *"sculpture"* removed. It was the NSDAP that opposed the blasphemies in George Grosz's portfolio *"Ecce Homo"*—yet a Prussian court under a Centre Party justice minister acquitted Grosz!

The first act of Thuringia's National Socialist Minister of Education, Dr. Frick, was to reintroduce Christian school prayers, including prayers for Germany's reunification. The response was a storm of protest from Marxists and the Centre Party. Then a Reich court ruled these prayers—unconstitutional...

In Brunswick, Social Democrats had ruled unchallenged for years. In 1930, this state too gained a National Socialist minister. He reinstated school prayers for both Christian denominations, previously forbidden. The Centre Party, long allied with atheistic Marxism in Prussia, saw no need to pressure its Brunswick comrades on this issue. Securing political advantage outweighed all else.

When the Centre Party now brazenly claims that National Socialism is organizing a new"culture war"—i.e., preparing state persecution of the Catholic Church—this is a malicious lie of the worst kind. However individual National Socialists may regard this or that religious dogma, they have always rejected any power-political interference against a denomination and will continue to do so. They have proven this through action. The Centre Party has done the opposite: it has defended Catholic dogmas with words while enabling-unbridled atheist propaganda through its alliances with Marxism, thereby rendering service to Bolshevism as a whole. Thus, the prerequisite for religious renewal is the destruction of Marxism and the downfall of the Centre Party as long as it actively fosters Marxism in practice.

On the Protestant side, similarly opportunistic political adventurers have observed the growth of the anti-Marxist movement. They have now founded a confessional party akin to the Centre: the Christian-Social People's Service.

There can be no doubt that National Socialism takes precisely the same stance toward this *"Protestant"* creation as it does toward the *"Catholic"* Centre. Greater success for the *"People's Service"* would degrade Germany's great liberation struggle into a purely confessional matter, forcing the battle back onto a plane that must remain outside the grand political confrontation. Incidentally,the first act of this *"Evangelical"* Reichstag faction was to vote against the candidate of the national opposition for Reichstag president. They preferred instead to join the Centre Party in supporting the champion of war guilt denial—the left-wing Social Democrat Paul Löbe. Here too, then, outright betrayal of both national and Christian ideals.

Given this treacherous, purely materialistic stance by political representatives of both confessions, it is no wonder that church resignations proliferate, that sects like the Adventists and Bible Students swell enormously, or that Moscow's International of the Godless prepares organized destruction of all religious values with vast resources. Against these forces eroding the people, the NSDAP has taken action (even in Munich, the *"Bible Students'"* rallies were only banned by the Bavarian People's Party government after our German protests). Yet the very existence of these currents reveals the weakness of the inner persuasive power wielded by current representatives of both Catholic and Protestant churches.

Assessing deeper ideological causes here lies beyond the NSDAP's purview, but the movement considers it both an absolute right and an imperative duty to highlight one phenomenon: the advance of clergy into political party struggles. Bismarck himself reproached Stöcker for wanting to be both an active preacher and political leader,instinctively recognizing that national policy would inevitably be subordinated to confessional considerations, and that the psychology of a spiritual shepherd cannot be organically reconciled with that of a political combat leader. Today Germany again faces a party—the Centre Party—under purely clerical leadership. Its chairman and foreign policy spokesman (alongside Prelate Ulika) is the papal domestic prelate Dr. Kaas; the Bavarian People's Party's de facto leader is Cathedral Provost Wohlmut, head of its Bavarian parliamentary faction; while Dean Leicht leads its Reichstag faction and serves as foreign policy spokesman. The Catholic press apparatus rests largely with Prelate Müller, while Prelates Fassel, Father Muckermann S.J., and others shape public opinion for the Centre. Clergyman Dr. Moenius (editor of the *"Allgemeine Rundschau"*) considers it his *"Catholic"*task to *"break the backbone"* of (German) nationalism and prevent formation of a German nation-state (*"Paris is France's heart"*). Thus Catholic priests spearhead the Centre's political battles (while patriotic clergy like Abbot Schachleitner and Dr. theol. Haeuser are simply forbidden to speak), and when opponents criticize the Centre's destructive policies by rejecting these leaders, it is branded—*"priest-baiting."*

Here again Italy—acting on papal orders—has set an example. During liberalism's ascendancy, the priest Don Sturzo led the liberal-Catholic Popular Party (the so-called Popolari Party). A fierce Fascist opponent who accused it (echoing German Centre prelates) of *"violating the nation,"* Don Sturzo was checked in 1923 when the Vatican forbade all priests political activity. Pope Pius XI officially declared: "There is no Catholic party, nor can there be one. Catholic principles and political rights find protection and interpretation within the Church itself.[2]" This pronouncement implies either multiple interchangeable Catholic worldviews,or—where political-material interests are at stake—the Centre disregards papal views too. Since Catholics cannot accept the first, they must conclude the latter, casting Centre leaders(loyal comrades of Matthias Erzberger, whom they still praise) in a damning light. The"Augsburger Postzeitung"—a leading southern German Centre paper and vitriolic opponent of Germany's freedom movement—felt compelled to admit that *"Neo-Paganism"*(the Centre's

---

2 Particularly noteworthy in this context is the judgment of Rome's *"Beritas"*correspondence (No.3, dated January 17, 1931), published by a personal friend of PopePius X. It states verbatim: *"The political hucksters (brocanteurs) of Catholicism—Sturzo, Sangnier, Strathmann with their gangs (bandes), the German Centre Party, its allied Bavarian People's Party, and all their ilk (tutti quanti)— impose no restraints in their unsavory associations. Consider Bavarian People's Party deputy Martin Loibl, who secritical party organ, the 'Neuburger Anzeigeblatt,' published an advertisement for a Communist rally. It reads verbatim: 'Communist Party of Germany, Third Group...Speaker... But what are the good priests, the pupils and recruiters of the party actually doing? Do they say nothing? Are they hypnotized or are they traitors?'"*

new term for National Socialism) now presents itself idealistically and heroically. It omitted only that many called to priestly office—to preach a kingdom not of this world—are increasingly dragged into materialism through political activity, forfeiting their exemplary role. The people sense this everywhere, partly explaining why anti-religious criticism finds fertile ground. The task of Centre prelates is not delivering Catholic lip-service at rallies before dividing political spoils with atheistic Marxist allies, but leaving the political arena to become what they were ordained to be: pastors. Today Germany needs Erzberger's human manure less than ever, but note how the Centre's hateful spirit has infiltrated even outwardly apolitical circles. It can for instance, a Bavarian priest openly slandered Adolf Hitler from the pulpit, claiming he had desecrated a Eucharistic host. Though convicted of defamation, the priest was acquitted. Thus, Centre Party priests enjoy immunity for slander! In the diocese of Würzburg, children are threatened with severe penalties and hellfire for attending National Socialist rallies or reading the 'Völkischer Beobachter.' Women are told to deny marital relations to husbands who refuse to vote for the Centre Part, etc. All this—combined with vicious harassment of clergy who refuse to agitate for the Centre—outrages the healthy sensibilities of a people who increasingly see their pastors transformed into narrow-minded Centre Party hacks.

The 1931 conflict between Fascism and Catholic Action brought particularly notable clarification. Catholic Action was accused—based on embarrassing revelations—of smuggling anti-Fascist leaders, comrades of Don Sturzo, into its newspaper and organizing conspiracies against the Italian state system. A bitter press feud erupted. Negotiations commenced, culminating in a September 1931 settlement.

The new agreement between the Italian government and the Vatican regarding Catholic Action bears all the marks of fierce mutual struggle over every inch of contested advantage. Yet neither party wished to risk rupture, and in the final protocol both waived dogmatic definitions of their differing views on Italian youth education. Practically speaking, the Vatican conceded nearly everywhere, while Mussolini fully permitted Catholic Action's religious activities—as before. By relinquishing Catholic Action's social organizations and even sports programs, the Vatican abandoned its claimed right to societal(social) influence, ceding the field entirely to Fascism. This implicitly admits that contrary to *"L'Osservatore Romano's"* claims, Catholic Action had previously engaged in state politics—now categorically prohibited. Locally, it's further stipulated that Catholic Action must maintain purely religious character, employ no lay editors, and be led exclusively by clergy unopposed to Fascism. Beyond clearly delimiting Catholic Action's scope, the state thus secured veto power against attempts to smuggle remnants of Don Sturzo's faction (the Italian Centre Party comrades) into Catholic Action publications. This provision compels the Vatican to purge Catholic Action's leadership—a cleansing the government will undoubtedly monitor rigorously.

The new accord also strips Catholic Action of all symbolism: the sole flag permitted alongside purely religious emblems is the Italian national tricolor. This is no trivial matter,for when Catholic Action marches under the same banner as Fascists, it creates a unifying element—favoring the state.

These provisions hold transnational significance, embodying programmatic content without doctrinal disputes: the agreement clarifies relations between the nation-state and Roman Church amid 20th-century realities. Where the Vatican once claimed global political dominion, later formally renounced politics, then defended against accusations of state interference, it now acknowledges—as essential for civic peace—that its subordinate associations may operate only within ecclesiastical-religious bounds, not even social-organizational ones, and must be led solely by individuals unobjectionable to state-sanctioned nationalism.

Doubtless Mussolini secured these concessions only because the Vatican—facing"Spanish"-language revelations in *"Il Lavoro Fascista"* about its high officials' anti-Fascist conspiracy—felt legally vulnerable and feared failed negotiations might spark a conflict risking, given Italy's broader unrest, still greater losses of prestige at minimum.

For his part, Mussolini prudently halted anti-Vatican press campaigns to preserve his state's international maneuverability, keeping avenues for peaceful resolution open. He avoided humiliating concessions and softened the appearance of Vatican retreat by emphasizing the desirability of church-led religious education—embraced by nearly all Italians.

When the Fascist press declared that Peter had received his due and Caesar his rightful claim, this reflected sound Christian interpretation. It follows that this luminous distinction must prevail elsewhere—eliminating *"culture wars,"* safeguarding all faiths' freedom of conscience, and restoring the state as the organized national community defending law and collective future, irrespective of individuals' metaphysical or philosophical leanings.

Religious renewal cannot occur until German priests recommit to their true office,submitting to their church superiors' decrees and agreements.

The same naturally applies to Protestants. The Protestant parsonage in small towns and villages undoubtedly represented Protestantism's finest cultural flowering. Here too, the world city has exerted its nerve-wracking influence, awakening ambitions that once channeled energies purely toward pastoral care. Here too, the clergyman—so long as he serves as such—should vanish from parliamentary murk and refrain from political mass gatherings.

We seek neither to constrain the Lutheran nor the Catholic cleric in his vitality: but from the pulpit, and in the manner his universal office demands, he should address only what is nationally collective, socially universal, and culturally overarching (at most extending to large popular assemblies). Herein lie the great possibilities for impact, herein alone the levers to deepen and renew religious life. It is as unnatural for a pastor to become a parliamentarian as for a statesman to assume the confessional. The organic delineation of spheres is the foundational premise for Germany's spiritually sound reconstruction—countless misunderstandings and conflicts would never arise.

National Socialism's state philosophy could only welcome genuine religious sentiment; the conflict arises solely because churches—particularly the uniformly international Roman Catholic hierarchy—expand the religious domain to encompass the social and thereby the political. National Socialism cannot alter this stance of a hierarchical center beyond Germany's borders; its state duty lies solely in ensuring, through church treaties, that governance remains free from ecclesiastical interference as much as from class or estate interests. It must not, for foreign policy convenience, grant greater rights to one-third Catholic citizens than to two-thirds Protestants. Moreover, it must utterly dispense with talk of *"parity"* in appointments. Favoring political positions based on religious affiliation fosters corruption of conviction and administration. In the coming state, appointments will be made solely by merit in service to the national whole. Though human fallibility can never be fully eliminated, striving to uphold this principle alone can guarantee maximum justice and spur the individual's legitimate ambition.

The National Socialist state is fundamentally prepared to conclude treaties with religious communities. Protestant and Catholic representatives stand before it as equals, though the state must reserve final authority over critical educational matters as its unquestionable right. Should agreement prove impossible, the future Reich will unilaterally regulate church-state relations with perfect religious tolerance—indeed, protecting religious life while eliminating denominational encroachment on state politics. Viewed through this clear lens, the Vatican too may one day find it expedient to reach firm agreements. The era when a church presumed to dictate laws to states has passed, despite the considerable power still wielded in many places. The 1931 tensions between Vatican and Fascism, events in Catholic Spain, even small Italy's stance toward the Vatican, and the national-Catholic tendencies among Czechs—all are symptoms of a radical völkisch spiritual upheaval. Should the Roman Church persist in attitudes like Cardinals Faulhaber's and Bertram's condemnations of German nationalism, then Germany's national Catholics too will understand the necessity of securing the state—upon whose strength their political and economic destiny depends.

National Socialism approaches the church-state problem not dogmatically but pragmatically, resolving it according to future realities. Those willing to give the people what they need for their struggle of self-assertion can coexist peacefully with the National Socialist state. Those unwilling must bear the consequences.

CHAPTER

5

REBIRTH OF CIVILIZATION

Just as in religion, the NSDAP cannot—beyond certain fundamentals—bind its members to detailed cultural doctrines, for art, philosophy, scientific convictions must necessarily reflect diverse temperaments. Often, an artist's dogmatic defense of his vision or a scholar's exclusive adherence to his theory contains the very essence of creative power. Nevertheless, cultural policy remains one of National Socialism's most vital domains—today as a political movement, tomorrow as state foundation and Reich government. For all class improvement, racial betterment, and physical hygiene remain half-measures without parallel soul-hygiene, without spiritual forces revitalizing petrified life to initiate true,profound rebirth. Here, while respecting personal cultural convictions, we must look forward and declare:

Germany's political-economic collapse was no mere external event: it mirrored an inner faithlessness toward Germanness and its promised mission; hence, German politics' aimlessness reveals a lack of national-popular, state, and cultural ideals. Simplification, abandonment, inner fragmentation, and hopelessness thus mark many Germans concerned for their people's spiritual heritage.

Most tasked with defending and creatively renewing German intellectual life pursued two phantasms: the self and so-called humanity. That between these lay blood-bound nationhood was often accepted almost shamefully as a necessary condition, seldom as the indispensable premise of all creation. Today, all counter forces have triumphed—those advocating politically for a world republic (or Pan-Europe), culturally for a rootless"humanity-culture" devoid of folk-consciousness. The individual is thus culturally severed from race, people, state, language, and history, theoretically amalgamated with hundreds of millions across nations and continents...

Just as today's international economic system places naked profit-seeking at the center of all its endeavors, so too the true driving force behind the sermon of humanity is unleashed greed—a doctrine enabling the individual to arrange his life and cultural work without obligation to people or state. Yet to cloak this naked materialism, one speaks of duty toward so-called humanity—an empty phrase, lacking any tangible entity. Despite this nearly omnipresent current, there grows an awareness that the complete victory of internationalism in its various forms would spawn not harmonious humanity nor"humanity-culture," but chaos across all spheres of life. The signs of our times scream this truth daily. In all nations, awakening forces now labor to counterbalance this—witness Germany, where organic creative will prepares for spiritual revolt in many places independently. We firmly believe this defense against chaos, this awakening to the primal truth of blood-bound nationhood and social obligation, will mature into mythical force. This faith—despite all—gives us courage. To lend aim, form, and substance to these still-scattered forces is our era's great task for salvaging our spiritual future.

Today, from the gutters of pestilential world-cities, the subhuman has emerged. Millions of wretchedly uprooted souls are cast onto asphalt—space-starved, denationalized, directionless—prey to every gaudy race-defiler who dares present mulatto and negro cultures as the highest achievement of the modern spirit. They are the harbingers of decay, akin to the internationalist Hellenists of degenerate Greece or the Syrian-African pacifist salons of dying Rome.

However diverse past cultures, Fichte's words unveil Germanic Europe's essence: *"Our culture is a culture of character."* Herein lies the driving force of all our cultural creations—for character-values underpin all societal preconditions for cultural creativity, and motivate Germanic life-shaping and ancient legal sensibilities. None grasp this more clearly than the born enemy of racial culture: the aforementioned concentrated dregs of world-cities—the intellectual and non-intellectual subhuman rabble under Jewish leadership that now influences and commands millions, already launching assaults in places, laboring daily to universalize this. This assault on all European—especially Germanic—cultural values is somewhat masked politically, where *"social demands"* still drown out destructive aims, and political movements can feign *"objectivity,"* since tactical disagreements may seem justified for survival. But in culture, this destructive fury stands naked, demonstrable across all fields with terrifying clarity. It is—in short—the instinctive and often conscious campaign to overthrow all values defining Germanic-German culture, transcending mere social and political collapses.

Every active German knows how far the gagging of intellectual freedom and cultural foundations has progressed—yet too many believe this economic, un-German terror strangles only their own vocation. In truth, it reigns everywhere. The situation is crushingly dire—precisely why it demands defiant resistance, to reclaim German spirit's dominion in its own house and make space for the fermenting powers of youth—poisoned from childhood beyond parents' ken. Recent trials should have roused all active minds.

The guilt is chiefly ours. And guilt demands atonement.

We atone passively through present intellectual misery: scholars barred from teaching at universities by ruling powers, while men forced upon German students insult front line soldiers and leaders. We atone as German artists are systematically supplanted by erotic sensationalists. We atone as German poets starve, cut off from their people by alien theaters and an international press-ring silencing vital forces. We atone as our legal system warps and faith in justice vanishes. This atonement is deserved—and will never change unless bearers of German essence in all classes rise to fight for intellectual and creative freedom. Many of the best, facing vile conditions, retreat despairingly into solitary work. But few can truly do so—most must serve their enemies. This very isolation of the valuable is what our foes seek, knowing withdrawal from active life equals surrender. This fragmentation of German cultural creators is among the deepest causes of our plight—but great calamities aren't overcome by piecemeal repairs, only when a new, organically rooted worldview takes up the fight, summoning those *"thousand hands"* without which even the noblest thoughts remain unrealized. That is—when national intellect steps boldly before the people it once estranged itself from.

True active atonement thus consists in defense, reclaiming genuine tradition, renewed creation from eternal folk-values, and shielding these emerging forces. To this end, all work must begin with oral and written enlightenment about the actual conditions, to overcome the appalling lack of insight, then awaken the feeling and will to resist all agents of decay—but also against one's own guilt and weakness. And finally, a forum must be created for the manifold, blood-bound German forces across all spheres of life.

In 1808, Baron vom Stein wrote to the Prussian king: *"If a warlike resolution is taken, remove all friends of peace, lest everything be paralyzed and halted in its forward movement."*

The spiritual turning point of our age is likewise contained in such a resolution. If it is not taken, all *"Germanness"* remains empty lip-service, spoken only to avoid betraying a faint and cowardly heart.

From this recognition of the overall situation, National Socialism must proceed—hence promoting everything in the cultural sphere that serves these insights, and combating everything that directly or indirectly submits to forces hostile to Germany. Engaged indecisive political struggle, the NSDAP initially lacked the means to divert its available forces toward gathering Germany's cultural creators. It later refrained as a whole, because meanwhile (1929) an organization had been founded whose aims National Socialism could trust: the *"Combat League for German Culture (Kampfbund für deutsche Kultur e.V.)"*, headquartered in Munich[1]. This League defined its purpose as follows:

"The Combat League for German Culture exists to defend the values of the German essence amidst today's cultural decay and to promote every racially authentic expression of German cultural life. The League aims to awaken the German people to the connections between race, art, and science, and to moral and volitional values. It aims to bring significant yet silenced Germans closer to the public through word and writing, thus serving cultural pan-Germanism without regard the artist and scholar is oft en "apolitical"—to some degree understandably, since creative power springs from specialized focus. Yet he must feel animated by the genius of his people and blood, sharply separating himself from those who deny this blood and seek to dissolve or bastardize it. This fundamental step has been taken by the Combat League for German Culture. A great number of Germany's creative forces have pledged themselves to it, enabling the emerging cultural and racial departments of the NSDAP to collaborate with it.

We know all too well today how closely power and culture are intertwined—hence we also know that cultural liberation is possible only by displacing the

---

1 Its Reich executive office is located in Munich, Barerstrasse 50, telephone 26 758, postal checking account Munich 16 481 to serve political boundaries. It sets itself the goal, through the unification of all forces that share these endeavors, of creating the prerequisite for an education in schools and universities that recognizes the national character of the people as the highest value. In particular, it sets itself the goal of awakening, in the growing generation of all strata of the people, an understanding of the nature and necessity of the struggle for the cultural and character values of the nation, and of strengthening the will for this struggle for German freedom."

current rulers who, as patrons of the Gumbels and Lessings, promote anti-German pseudo-culture through political means, exerting a terrible, soul-destroying influence. We therefore consider it the paramount task of every German-cultural association to identify, gather, and inspire genuinely creative workers in all fields—freeing them from feelings of abandonment—so that a future German ruler will know whom to appoint in place of those now misusing German souls in universities, academies, judges' benches, etc.

As a political combat organization, National Socialism has struck at culture's central battleground: the press (§23). Here it demands that all editors must be racial comrades;non-German newspapers require state approval to publish; and financial manipulation of German papers is prohibited. Further: *"We demand the legal prosecution of artistic and literary trends exerting a destructive influence on our national life, and the closure of events violating these demands."*

This outlines the great task in its static dimension: for the state, if it is not to strangle living life, can in cultural matters predominantly only act preventively—setting boundaries. Creativity remains always the domain of the individual. Yet it is decisive that state leadership consist of culturally creative, racially conscious individuals—not international market-forces, nor ossified bureaucrats or hypocritical moralists. For us, the focus is not commandments and prohibitions, but the human being.

If racial hygiene, coupled with racial improvement, is to create the physical precondition for recovery, the education system must immediately seize the German child's mind and soul—and here the NSDAP clashes violently with the old powers.

If we recognize that character sustains state and society, then the education of future Germans must above all mean character formation. Herein National Socialism fundamentally diverges from an intellectual trend of the past century that placed supreme value on knowledge. This intellectualize increasingly supplanted natural instinct,breeding an *"expert"* class devoid of a living, blood-bound center. Hence Germany produced so much *"objectivity"* and so little passionate advocacy of the national whole—hence even today, the German nation yields the greatest aircraft engineers, ingeniously designed pleasure craft, finest ocean liners, countless outstanding *"legal scholars,"* yet so few statesmen. In this light, Adolf Hitler's great political education was—viewed from the highest perspective—a literal rescue of character in Germany's darkest hour, undertaken by the German folk-soul. And since then, National Socialism has become the greatest folk-educator Germany has known since Frederick the Great and the men of 1813. He has brought awareness of the essence of human existence on this earth to millions, he has awakened the greatness of Germanic blood in millions more—in short, he has restored to the German nation, to its inventors and artists, its technicians and soldiers, their *"center of felicity"* (Herder), and given meaning back to all endeavor. But if this great deed is to continue shaping new generations—not to flare up briefly and then be forgotten—the National Socialist folk-state must demand one thing: the school! Against this demand, all those powers that have hitherto ruled will rise in bitter opposition—powers to whose rule Germany owes its moral and, consequently, political decline. One such group, the Centre Party and large segments of orthodox Protestantism, ultimately demand church-run schools. For now, they still call them denominational schools, but what they mean is denominational segregation (*"Konfessionssilberung"*) extending even to natural science and—penmanship. Here, a clear separation is necessary. As previously stated, religion is an innermost matter of conscience concerning metaphysical questions, which no state is authorized to decide by coercive measures, let alone by decree. Only parents may judge in what form a child should receive religious instruction. And since religious views undeniably differ, denominational religious instruction is defensible even from the National Socialist standpoint—provided it is conditional that nothing may be undertaken which violates national consciousness. In all other subjects, however, the school's task is not to release Lutherans, Catholics, German-Christians (Deutsch-Fürstler), Reformed, etc., into life, but nationally and state-conscious Germans. Promoting purely denominational influence (particularly the church's meddling in rural areas) would sharpen the religious fragmentation of the people and sow the seeds for later, unavoidable civil discord(*"unabhängbare Zivilsitten"*).

The term *"simultaneous school,"* posed as an alternative to denominational schools, bears all the marks of purely liberalistic thinking, which fixates only on externals and schematics. For the spiritual counterpart to the denominational school and the simultaneous school is the German National School, which encompasses not a part but fixes its gaze on the whole. The simultaneous presence of Protestants, Catholics, etc., will therefore naturally be a prerequisite for all other school types, however differently structured they may otherwise be.

From this follows the task of re-framing history. It must not bear Catholic or Protestant dogmatic coloring but must proceed from the fact of blood, the diversity of races and racial souls; it must depict the struggle of Nordic blood in Greece and Rome, the Germanic essence in its manifestations, its strengths and weaknesses. And the standard of evaluation for this historical perspective will derive from whether a personality, a historical phenomenon, or an intellectual current has purified and strengthened or weakened the German essence. National Socialism will welcome all preliminary work in this field (Lagarde, Ranke, Treitschke, Wagner, Chamberlain, Krieck, Günther) and will continually seek out great educators of the people, so that their worth does not remain mere words or literature, but becomes vital, living reality.

In the thorough penetration of all problems, the National Socialist Teachers' League works in a comprehensive manner, and the final programmatic elaboration of all principles will be the task of all the pedagogical forces of this organization[2].

The same applies to the realm of law. §19 of our program demands in thesis form the fundamental replacement of the current Jewish-Roman legal system with a German common law. Even in shaping such a law, certain differences over details will need to be overcome. But one principle stands out for us as paramount: that the future German law must above all be a law of duty. The

---

2   Office: Munich, Briennerstraße 45.

liberalistically inclined generation did not proceed from the rights of the collective—which first enables the individual's civic existence and protects it—but catastrophically shifted the weight of legal theory to this individual. To be sure, the organically developed institutions of a healthier past—the army and civil service—still held firm, and cultural tradition still forged souls together. Nevertheless, just as politically through race-less democracy, so too in the legal sphere the superfluous was treated as self-evidently justified, and nearly all objects it dealt with were degraded into commodities. *"Every owner of a thing may deal with it as he pleases,"* states a famous paragraph of the Civil Code (§903). This is the inversion of the ancient German legal principle that the common good takes precedence over private benefit—a principle prominently emphasized in §24 of the NSDAP program, which establishes the movement's religious stance. Indeed, within this inner attitude toward the question of right and duty lies the value of genuine religious feeling—rooted. It leads directly to Immanuel Kant's grandly simple formula: *"Morality is not properly the doctrine of how we make ourselves happy, but of how we may become worthy of happiness."* This inner pride elevates itself above the *"rights"* of the self to service in the realization of a sublime idea, and only in this way raises the person to true personality. Even if individuals sin against this principle countless times, the mere fact that they recognize it as valid for themselves and the state gives the collective its style, character, and constancy—making atonement and eradication by this collective appear as necessary consequences when someone impairs or destroys the collective's freedom. Under individualistic law, however, every profiteer views prosecutors and judges merely as nuisances interfering with his *"justified"* work of speculating to amass wealth, even over corpses. One step further and we arrive at the Social Democratic thesis that everyone must have the *"right"* to treason as well, which therefore must not be punished. (In the press of Marxist orientation, unpunished articles already appear where the author promises to denounce all known German armaments to foreign powers.) This shift in perspective leads directly to the Marxist concept of property. For what Marxism does in this and other cases is a brutal assault on national property—which consists of national freedom, state sovereignty, the ability to defend the nation's territory, and to represent its moral and material interests throughout the world. Thus there exists a sacred property in the highest sense, transcending all individual interests, to which everything else must subordinate it self as a function of this overarching idea!

From this standpoint, National Socialism draws the following conclusion: it recognizes lawfully acquired property, indeed in all spheres. An invention, a poetic work are property, just like the money saved through honest daily labor by a common man. But should a willful genius seek to exploit an invention against the collective people, this collective must render such actions harmless—just as it would suppress even the most brilliantly crafted drama promoting treason, or harmful speculation with honestly acquired money.

Where the concept of private property is restricted here, it will depend upon the stricter interpretation of the common good—again understood in the highest sense as the sum of the moral character values of collective existence. Graphically expressed: today's *"businessman"* can walk for kilometers before encountering a judge—if he meets one at all. But tomorrow, when the National Socialist state has overcome the current interregnum, this man will see the prosecutor before him after just a few steps on the profiteer's path. Whoever opposes this conception of private property thereby proves only that German concepts of honor and duty have burned out within him, replaced by Jewish concepts.

An even sharper stance toward private property is taken by the NSDAP regarding landownership. This must never be treated as a commodity—not the product of human invention or labor, but a piece of the cosmos, a vital prerequisite for the people's collective existence, defended for generations with their blood at the nation's borders. The National Socialist Gregor Strasser once beautifully formulated this relationship: when the unparalleled worker, student, artist, scholar—indeed, the urban dweller—defends with his body the soil of the farmer, the landowner, he thereby also earns the right to ensure that this defended land does not fall into decay, lie fallow, or worse, be bartered away to racially foreign outsiders. The farmer feeds the people; thus, the peasant is the foundation for the nation's very life, and this nation, organized as a state, protects both his freedom and the fruits of his labor. Therefore, land is not a commodity; it must never be an object of speculation. Indeed, the true people's state must reserve the right not only to convert private property into national property—with appropriate compensation—for necessary public purposes, but also, when the collective is severely harmed, to expropriate without compensation. All this together constitutes the meaning of our profoundly justified §17—so furiously opposed by the entire liberalist world—to which Adolf Hitler provided a brief commentary in 1928, later supplemented by an agrarian program in March 1930 (seeappendix).

School and law—these are the great levers of national awakening. Press and literature(today also film and radio) are means of influencing the public, which must remain under vigilant supervision. The liberal notion of *"freedom of the press"* stands on the same level as demanding freedom to distribute not just wholesome nourishment but all poisons. H.S Chamberlain already drew the comparison: just as the state establishes market police to protect citizens from harmful consumables, so too must it guard against attempts to poisonous spiritually. Today's *"state"* has indeed introduced protective laws—not to safeguard national honor or racial health, but to shield the current *"form of government"* and its deceased and living ministers. (Under such a law, a Marxist provincial governor even banned a newspaper for publishing a caricature of Wirth.) Thus, all the Eisners, Erzbergers, Hoefles, Bauers, Scheidemanns, Eberts, and countless other ministerial figures enjoy protective paragraphs, while it remains permissible and popular to call Germania a whore(Lichnowsky), or to portray the German army as desecrators of sacraments and murderers of Belgians—a sport pursued with impunity especially by Centre Party leaders (Pastor Föry, Dr. Mönius). For the rest, National Socialism is no friend of a police state where the word *"forbidden"* appears everywhere. It wholly embraces a system where police presidents or prudish clubs may rage against *"immorality"* or violently interfere with artistic expression. Yet we do advocate forming a cultural council within the National Socialist Order (or Senate), composed of incorruptible, sensitive individuals empowered to disseminate the movement's cultural perspectives through press, radio, etc., while also ensuring struggling artists across all fields retain the means to express their ideas. Here rests National Socialism's faith in German vitality. Once the people are detoxified by removing racial enemies, once these opponents of German rebirth are denied opportunities for racial contamination, the hypnosis by *"world papers,"* Jewish cinemas, and radio bastards will gradually fade, replaced by unbiased judgment—hand in hand with a general purification of public life[3].

We leave to the future the specific forms our cultural work will take in theater, visual arts,poetry, etc. Today, we focus only on those who must one day be expelled from the sacred institutions of German education, German legal life, from directorial posts and academies—and we note those who have gifted us German values, or who, as a young generation,visibly strive to shape these values.

And then—free rein to the healthy, creative German.

---

3 I have elaborated further on the essence of Germanic art in the second book of my *"Mythof the 20th Century."*

CHAPTER

6

SYMBOLS OF LIFE

Man cannot grasp and depict the world, life, in their immediacy. The essence of life is its uninterrupted activity, while the essence of human spirit and consciousness is the interrupted, the intermittent. Without this mental pause, not a single work of art, not a single formulated scientific thought, not one heroic deed would be possible. This profound distinction between the ceaseless, flowing organic life process and the nature of our comprehension compels us to further discern and bring to consciousness those forms through which man appropriates the world, subordinates it, or serves it.

Perception acts most immediately, either convincing or provoking rejection. We can only attain understanding of the present problem through a framework of reason, while man is driven by the spur of will. Perception always operates according to its eternal laws through symbols. Whoever has stood before the tomb of Frederick the Great and Frederick William I in Potsdam's Garrison Church, whoever has consciously gazed upon the old tattered Prussian banners on the walls—from these symbolic flag fragments an entire world arises for them: the greatest epochs of German history, the greatest parables of German strength and sacrificial courage. A new symbol, too, is what the National Socialist Movement today carries through the streets of German villages and cities in endless repetition. This symbol shows us directly in color and design what we know theoretically and desire inwardly. Around this symbol, day by day, month by month, year by year, new thoughts, new values,new sacrifices continually gather—so that not only the new banner itself becomes a symbol, but also the men who bear these flags. Only those inwardly conditioned by the great values of Germanness and possessing the courage to uphold them outwardly can truly pledge themselves to this new emblem.

And here we can already discern a mystical correspondence between these character values and ideals with immediate perception—namely, that the average of any humanity fighting alongside us in our ranks also acknowledges a racial ideal, just as unbiased ages proclaimed through their art. A racial ideal that intimately connects the great female figures of the Parthenon pediment in Athens with Gudrun's folds and Goethe's Dorothea, just as it links Greek male figures with the Germanic ideal of beauty still upheld in our own day.

A flag, a sign becomes holier the longer battles have been fought beneath it; within it is embodied the immutability of an idea, no matter how many thousands of different hands have clenched their fists around the flagstaff. Alongside the genius-simple formulation of our era's thought, I consider it Adolf Hitler's greatest deed to have gifted National Socialism with a banner that directly and visibly symbolizes the greatness of Germanic essence—absorbing and carrying forward all sacrifices and victories for the idea. The black-white-red colors recall those flags under which Germany marched into holy war in 1914 to protect people and homeland from the stranglehold of the eternal enemy in the West. But the swastika suddenly vaults across centuries, millennia, pointing to the very sources of that strength from which German creative deeds once sprang. In times when this emblem traveled the world as a sign of Nordic blood, it became a symbol of fertility and ascending life. True, this symbol traces back to *"heathen"* times—but National Socialism has no intention of denying the unity of Germanic-German essence or beginning German history with Charlemagne. However much of value may later have flowed into German nature from without, the core of all possibilities was present when the Germanic man first opened his eyes. And the swastika shall embody this unity for us.

A fierce struggle has erupted against this symbol from the obscurantists of our time—particularly the leaders of the Centre Party (who continually betray us to atheistic Marxism, to Poles and Frenchmen)—who have the audacity to slander this emblem in the name of Christianity, claiming it reduces us to the level of Ashanti Negroes.

Let us briefly follow these gentlemen (whose moral standards are evident throughout the Centre Party's press) and apply the same logic to the Roman Church, which they claim to defend as 100 percent anti-pagan and Christian.

First, there is the Christmas celebration: an ancient Germanic holiday of the winter solstice;likewise, St. John's Day: the pagan festival of the summer solstice. Constantine introduced Sunday and Christmas as a worshiper of Helios, since they were Helios-days. For Easter,Christianity not only borrowed the name of the Germanic spring goddess Ostara but also her symbolism of resurrection from winter's night, along with her emblem of the egg as a sign of fertility. And if these gentlemen wage war against totem-ism, they should truthfully admit that St.

Oswald and St. Martin represent nothing but renaming of Wotan, complete with his same symbols—cloak and spear.

Telling in this entire dishonest campaign of vilifying the swastika is the attempt to portray it as a distortion of the Christian cross. This effort reveals that the preachers of Christian churches lack even the faintest notion of the origin of the symbol they wear on their chests their entire lives. The swastika, a symbol born in the heart of Europe, is one of many celestial and solar signs. The sky and sun were depicted as a circle, as a wagon wheel with spokes, as an equilateral cross, as a swastika. From central Europe, this latter symbol migrated to Greece, where Schliemann discovered it in Troy (dating to around 2500 B.C.).From there, it spread with Nordic hosts as a sign of organically awakening life to India,where it first appeared around 500 B.C. and later became Buddha's second-holiest emblem. With Buddhism, the swastika reached China, where (enclosed in a circle) it symbolizes infinity. In another direction, Germanic peoples carried it to England, Nordic bands to Rome. In the catacombs, we find the swastika alongside the so-called Christian cross—both sharing the same origin and meaning. The Christian cross as a sign of the Roman torture stake was entirely unknown for over 200 years; indeed, as late as the 3rd century, Minutius Felix railed against the pagan *"Christian"* cross, until resistance to this symbol became untenable and Christ's torture stake (which was T-shaped, not cruciform) was declared the ineradicable emblem.

Alongside the *"Christian"* cross, the swastika persisted until the 16th century on bishops' miters, coins, altar cloths, cathedral chests—even today in Catholic prayer books (Beuron Benedictine Prayer Book)—and is still carved in stone on the communion rail and window tracery of the main facade of St. Martin's Church in Trier, built in 1912. Yet when the German freedom movement revives the ancient Germanic symbol in its original sense—as a profession of creative action, of blood and folk hood—a supposedly enlightened press rages about *"paganism."* We pose the reverse question: Is it Christian when the *"Catholic"*

Centre Party delivers all power in crosses to atheistic Social Democracy? Is it Christian when the Centre Party nominates the chairman of Berlin's Jewish religious community, the Zionist Kareski, as a Reichstag candidate? Is it Christian when international godless conventions can be held in Berlin under the watchful eyes of Centre Party men?

What peculiar Christianity this would be, if one had the audacity to proclaim such actions as Christian politics!

"Yet—it happens. Meanwhile, a German awakening emerges, yearning once more for purity and honor. And therefore, solely for this reason, the Centre Party's struggle against us rages as never before. But even this campaign of obfuscation will eventually meet it send. And our opponents notice the immense unifying power radiating from the swastika banner—against which they have nothing left to counter."

The swastika need not stand in opposition to the Christian cross. The NSDAP has never fought against the cross as such; it remained for the Centre Party alone to vilify the *"pagan symbol"* from the outset, to deny and besmirch the values of blood. Thus this party is well on its way to transforming the Christian cross into an emblem of empty racial rhetoric. The fault lies not with us if ecclesiastical authorities fail to resist this misuse of a religious world symbol for unclean party-political ends.

Christianity is a religious symbol, the swastika a racial-political battle emblem. Herein lies the distinction (and complementarity) between both symbols, clearly expressed by the NSDAP for anyone still of good will. When Catholic and Protestant SA men sought to attend their confession's churches with their banners, priests occasionally admitted them in earlier times—but in most cases turned them away. Today, the state flag bearing the Fascist symbol—undoubtedly also a *"pagan"* emblem from pre-Christian antiquity—stands beside the high altars of Italy's Catholic churches. The Italian Pope has raised no objections to this, nor to the playing of the royal anthem on Italian church organs. What is right for one Catholic should be fair for another. If bitterness arises among Italian circles in Germany against ecclesiastical authorities who vehemently storm against National Socialism and bar the symbol of German rebirth from houses of worship, the blame must be directed at the responsible Church officials.

Every expression of our life that seeks to manifest something internal is ultimately symbolic. All letters, all words, language itself are invented and recognized similitudes,emblems of a delimited community—mediating symbols to bridge the unbridgeable gap between inner essence and external appearance. Sound belongs here too, but above all color, line, and drawing. However refined and multifaceted the instrument of language and writing may be: the eye remains the most immediate tool through which we touch and comprehend the external world. A visual symbol will always carry more power than rational conscious agreement, because an emblem of light speaks directly from the eye to the soul, to the will. And as long as this holds true, the soul remains healthy.

At the time these lines are written, the NSDAP counts 200 men who have sealed their loyalty to the coming Reich with their lives. They did not fall in open frontal battle—they were ambushed from behind during their service to the Movement by Red Front, Reichs banner (and more recently by the Centre Party's *"Cross Brigade"*), shot dead,trampled by trains. They were thrown from their bicycles returning home from rallies,hunted down in their homes, had their eyes gouged out (cf. Senft) and murdered. The red press of the North published names and addresses of our SA and SS men to aid criminal elements—and so they all died: Kämmerer, Hirschmann,Wessel, Thielisch, Bobis, Steinbach, Garthe... Mostly poor laborers whose sole crime was loving Germany more than themselves.

Alongside these dead, over 8,000 SA and SS men bear the wounds of this terrible civil war upon their bodies—wounds sustained in countless ambushes raging across Germany,unreported by the bourgeois press. Nearly 50 wounded daily were counted in September1931—while the Jewish press of Berlin and Frankfurt only intensified their mockery.

And beside these men, we honor the National Socialist women to whom our idea and the swastika symbol give the strength to send forth their husbands, sons, and brothers each day,never knowing if they'll return. This quiet heroism shows we've overcome the spirit of November 1918 and entered a new heroic epoch for the German people. Within the National Socialist Movement—slandered as *"anti-woman"* by all 'righteous' critics—the German woman has regained her self-awareness. The great experience has freed her from ridiculous constraints and overrefined affectations of personality, but also from those literary ladies who now waste their useless existence as objects of ridicule in parliamentary clubs. True dignity has been restored by the NSDAP, and the German women in our movement know their men fight for their freedom and honor too. The future will prove how desperately Germany needs these National Socialist women.

In conclusion, some examples that themselves become symbols:

In Tyrol, a Hitler Youth lies mortally wounded by a communist's bullet to the head. A priest arrives to administer last rites—but demands he renounce Hitler. The brave youth,wrestling with death, refuses... He recovered and fights on today.

In late 1930, SA man Friedrich Weinstein was ambushed by communists and stabbed to death with knives. In his comrades' arms, his last words were: *"Hitler, I gladly die for you...Mother, I'm dying."* During our Saxon Gau Party Congress in Chemnitz (June 1931), Pg. Edgar Steinbach was shot dead by communists; Pg. Heinrich Gutsche mortally wounded. Adolf Hitler visited the dying man. Recognizing the Führer, he summoned strength to raise his riddled body, lifted his hand in final salute, gasped *"Heil Hitler"*—and died.

That same June, an SA unit in Bremen was overwhelmed by communist attackers. Defending their banner as they retreated, 31-year-old laborer and SA man Josef L. fell. His final wish was to be buried in Braunschweig.

In August 1931, National Socialists returning home in Limbach (Saxony) were fired upon by communists. Pg. Herbert Große, aged 23, was fatally wounded. His last words expressed the hope that the Third Reich might soon be established.

These are primal testimonies of Germanic-German character. They spring not only from eternally loyal peasant soil—no, what is truly monumental—they emerge from impoverished, light-less workers' dwellings. From nature-alienating, character-corrupting metropolises come these stammering cries of unshakable loyalty, that profound sense of allegiance awakened to life through Leader and banner: a shattering myth in our seemingly myth-less, essence-deprived era hostile to all nobility. This sacrifice for a future visible only in broad outlines is religion itself.

True religion isn't outward acceptance of dogmas, ecclesiastical claims, or traditional practices—but wherever a man bravely serves highest values, there is God, there the metaphysical becomes manifest in man. Death need not prove this—life itself does, though death brings this lived religion to fullest consciousness. Yet those who accompany a mass murderer (like Kürten) to the scaffold with all church rites, while denying ecclesiastical burial to a believing, honorable man who selflessly served his people (like National Socialist Gemeinber, who died of heart failure after a rally) because he served his people *"in our camp"*—such men stand not with God but with the devil.

The struggle waged by the National Socialist Movement thus transcends mere church affiliation—it is lived religion, metaphysics in action. All religious denominations to which these National Socialists belong (Protestants, Catholics, German Christians etc.) receive through them new impulses, an influx of higher values. They should thank them, not—as often occurs—revile and persecute them.

Regardless, the NSDAP wages its struggle not on grounds of ecclesiastical confession, but in battle against the powers of racial chaos, the rootless, those destroying the Volk. Here the swastika stands as today's sole true opponent to the Soviet star—symbol not just of Bolshevism but of all systems and men who prepared it intellectually and politically: Liberalism, Social Democracy and the Centre Party.

The swastika knows nothing of bourgeois satiety's former pleasures and symbols. It doesn't value peace above struggle—it esteems struggle itself as the creative birth of culture and true statehood.

Witnesses to this are those graves that have received our dead, those hundreds of thousands now facing a snarling Red Front daily while knowing treacherous cowards at their backs. Alongside the iron letters of our Leaders, these names are inscribed in the book of German history. I conclude with words spoken by an SA leader at the grave of our murdered Düsseldorf SS man Bobs: *"Sleep well, comrade, in dark earth! Soon brown battalions with waving banners and iron tread will thunder over graves, avenging you, conquering the Reich for which you fell."*

CHAPTER

7

APPENDIX (PROGRAM)

The German Workers' Party program addresses its time. The leaders reject establishing new goals after achieving the program's aims merely to artificially stimulate mass dissatisfaction and perpetuate the party's existence.

1. We demand the unification of all Germans based on self-determination into a Greater Germany.

2. We demand equality for the German people among nations, and abolition of the Versailles and St. Germain treaties.

3. We demand land and soil (colonies) to feed our people and settle our population surplus.

4. Only national comrades can be citizens. Only those of German blood, regardless of creed, qualify. No Jew can therefore be a national comrade.

5. Non-citizens may live in Germany only as guests under alien legislation.

6. Only citizens may determine state leadership and laws. We demand all public offices—whether Reich, state or municipal—be held exclusively by citizens.

We combat the corrupt parliamentary practice of appointing officials based solely on party affiliation without regard to character and ability.

7. The state must prioritize citizens' livelihood. If unable to feed the entire population,foreign nationals (non-citizens) must be expelled from the Reich.

8. Further non-German immigration must be prevented. We demand all non-Germans who entered Germany after August 2, 1914 be immediately compelled to leave the Reich.

9. All citizens must have equal rights and duties.

10. Every citizen's primary duty must be productive mental or physical labor. Individual activity must not violate communal interests but occur within the framework of the whole and for the benefit of all.

Therefore we demand:

11. Abolition of unearned income.

Breaking of interest slavery.

12. Given war's immense sacrifices of property and blood, personal war profiteering constitutes a crime against the people. We demand complete confiscation of all war profits.

13. We demand nationalization of all previously socialized industries.

14. We demand profit-sharing in major industries.

15. We demand expanded old-age welfare.

16. We demand creation/maintenance of a healthy middle class: immediate municipalization of department stores with affordable rental to small businesses; strongest consideration for all small businesses in government contracts.

17. We demand land reform adapted to our national needs, creation of a law for the expropriation of land without compensation for public purposes. Abolition of land speculation and prevention of all land profiteering[1].

18. We demand ruthless combat against those who harm communal interests through their activities. Common criminals, usurers, profiteers etc. shall be punished with death, without regard to creed or race.

19. We demand replacement of Roman Law serving the materialist world order with a German Common Law.

20. To enable every capable and diligent German to attain higher education and thus enter leading positions, the state must thoroughly expand our entire public education system.

Curricula of all educational institutions shall be adapted to practical life requirements. Comprehension of state concepts must begin with school instruction (civics). We demand state-funded education for intellectually gifted children of poor parents regardless of social status or occupation.

21. The state must safeguard public health by protecting mothers and children,

---

1 Regarding this program point, Adolf Hitler issued the following clarification on April 13,1928:

Declaration.

Against the fraudulent interpretations of Point 17 of the NSDAP program by our opponents, the following clarification is necessary.

Since the NSDAP stands on the basis of private property, it follows that the phrase"expropriation without compensation" refers solely to creating legal means to confiscate land acquired unlawfully or not administered for the public good—primarily targeting Jewish land speculation companies.

Munich, April 13, 1928.

Signed, Adolf Hitler.

prohibiting child labor, instituting compulsory physical education through gymnastics and sports, and vigorously supporting all youth athletic associations.

22. We demand abolition of mercenary troops and creation of a national army.

23. We demand legal combat against deliberate political lies and their dissemination through the press. To create a German press, we demand that:

a) all editors and contributors of German-language newspapers must be national comrades,

b) non-German newspapers require explicit state permission. They may not be printed in German,

c) any financial participation in or influence over German newspapers by non-Germans shall be prohibited, with penalties including closure of such newspaper operations and immediate expulsion of involved non-Germans from the Reich.

Newspapers violating public welfare shall be banned. We demand legal combat against artistic and literary tendencies exerting destructive influence on national life, and closure of events violating these principles.

24. We demand freedom for all religious denominations in the state, provided they don't endanger its existence or offend the moral sensibilities of the Germanic race.

The party as such represents positive Christianity without binding itself confessionally. It combats the Jewish-materialist spirit within and without, convinced that our nation's permanent recovery can only proceed from within on the principle:

Common good before private good.

25. To implement all this, we demand: Creation of strong central Reich authority. Absolute authority of the central parliament over the entire Reich and its general organization.

Formation of estates and vocational chambers to implement Reich food laws in federal states.

The party leadership pledges to enforce these points ruthlessly, sacrificing life itself if necessary.

Munich, February 24, 1920.

Signed, Adolf Hitler.

Official Party Proclamation.

Org. Dept. II.   Munich, March 1930.

1. The Peasantry and Agriculture's Role for the German People

The German people obtain considerable sustenance through imported foodstuffs. Before the World War, we paid for these imports with industrial exports, trade, and foreign investments. The war's outcome destroyed this possibility.

Today we pay for food imports largely with borrowed foreign money, sinking our people deeper into debt slavery to international high finance. Continued thus, they will increasingly enslave us—through credit embargoes and food supply stoppages, literally holding bread hostage to compel German proletarians either to work as starving serfs or be shipped as labor slaves to foreign colonies.

Liberation requires self-sufficiency through our own soil.

Increasing agricultural productivity has thus become a vital national question.

An economically healthy peasantry is equally crucial for marketing our industry's products as we focus increasingly on domestic markets.

We recognize the peasantry not only as our nutritional foundation, but as the mainstay of hereditary health, the nation's rejuvenating wellspring, and the bastion of defensive strength.

Maintaining a capable peasantry—numerically proportionate to growing population needs—forms a cornerstone of National Socialist policy, precisely because this policy serves the whole people's welfare for generations to come.

2. Disregard for the Peasantry and Agricultural Neglect in Present-Day Germany

Contrary to biological and economic necessities, and despite urgent needs for increased agricultural output, today's German state gravely threatens the preservation of an economically sound peasant class.

The substantial increase in agricultural production that would otherwise be possible is being prevented because the necessary operating resources are lacking due to farmers' mounting debts, and because the incentive for increased productivity is absent, as agricultural labor no longer proves profitable.

The causes of this insufficient remuneration (profitability) of agricultural work must be examined:

1. In current tax policies disproportionately burdening agriculture. This occurs due to partisan considerations and because the Jewish world power that actually governs German parliamentary democracy seeks the destruction of German agriculture, as this would leave the German people—particularly the working class—completely defenseless.

2. In competition from foreign agriculture producing under more favorable conditions,which is not sufficiently restrained by agricultural and foreign trade policies.

3. In the excessively high profits appropriated by Jewish-dominated wholesale trade in agricultural products, which currently lies mostly in Jewish hands, intervening between producers and consumers.

4. In the usurious prices farmers must pay for fertilizer and electricity to mostly Jewish-owned conglomerates.

The meager proceeds from underpaid agricultural labor can no longer cover high taxes. Farmers are compelled to incur debts, paying usurious interest, sinking deeper into interest slavery until they finally lose homes and farms to predominantly Jewish moneylenders.

The German peasantry is being uprooted.

3. In our envisioned future Reich, German land law shall prevail and German land policy be pursued

No fundamental improvement in rural distress or agricultural recovery can be expected while the German Reich remains governed through parliamentary democracy by international financial powers who seek to destroy Germany's rooted native forces.

Only in our envisioned fundamentally different new German state will peasants and agriculture assume their rightful role as a cornerstone of a true German national state.

In this future Reich, German land law shall prevail and German land policy be pursued.

This necessitates the following demands:

1. German soil, occupied and defended by the German people, serves the habitation and sustenance of the entire nation. It must therefore be administered solely in this spirit.

2. Only German national comrades may own German land.

3. Land legitimately acquired by German national comrades shall be recognized as hereditary property.

This property right is however bound to the obligation of using the land for the common good.

Monitoring this obligation shall be the duty of corporative courts composed of representatives from all occupational groups of the agricultural population and one state representative.

4. German soil must not become an object of financial speculation nor serve as unearned income for its owner. Henceforth, only those intending to cultivate land themselves may acquire it.

The state therefore holds the right of first refusal over all land sales.

Mortgaging land to private lenders is prohibited.

Necessary operating loans on favorable terms shall be provided to agriculture through its state-recognized corporative cooperatives or directly by the state.

5. For the use of German soil, owners shall pay the state a levy proportionate to the size and quality of their holdings. This land yield tax renders further state taxation of agricultural land and operations obsolete.

6. No schematic regulation can govern the size of agricultural operations.

From a population policy standpoint, maintaining numerous viable small and medium-sized farms is paramount.

Large-scale operations also fulfill essential specialized functions and are justified when proportionally balanced with medium and small holdings.

7. Land inheritance rights shall be regulated through single-heir succession laws to prevent land fragmentation and operational overburdening.

8. The state reserves the right of expropriation with fair compensation:

   a) for land not owned by German national comrades;
   b) for land that—per ruling by the competent corporative court—no longer serves the people's sustenance due to its owner's irresponsible mismanagement;
   c) for portions of large estates not personally cultivated by owners, to establish independent peasant holdings;

d) for land required by the national community for special state purposes (e.g.,transportation infrastructure, national defense). Illegitimately acquired land (as defined by German law) shall be expropriated without compensation.

9. Systematic settlement of available land—guided by broad demographic principles—is a state responsibility. Land shall be allocated to settlers as hereditary leases with initial conditions enabling viable farms.

Applicants shall be selected after assessing their civic and professional suitability for settlement. Special consideration shall be given to non-inheriting sons of farmers (see point7).

Borderland settlement in the East is particularly vital. This cannot be satisfactorily resolved merely through establishing farms, but requires developing regional market towns alongside industrial realignment—creating the self-sufficiency that ensures viability for newly established small and medium farms.

Securing extensive nutritional and settlement space for Germany's growing population is the task of German foreign policy.

4. The peasantry shall be economically and culturally elevated

The state must promote the economic and cultural advancement of the peasantry commensurate with its national importance, thereby addressing a primary cause of rural depopulation.

1. First, the current oppressive hardship of the rural population must be alleviated through tax relief measures and other special provisions. The further indebtedness of agriculture must be halted by legally reducing interest rates on borrowed capital to pre-war levels and through the most stringent measures against usury.

2. Through its economic policy, the state must ensure that agricultural labor becomes profitable once more.

Domestic agricultural production must be protected through tariffs, state-regulated imports,and purposeful national education.

Agricultural commodity pricing must be removed from stock exchange speculation, and the exploitation of farmers by wholesale trade must be prevented. The state shall promote the transfer of agricultural wholesale trade to agricultural cooperatives.

The competent agricultural organizations have the task of reducing production costs for farmers while increasing output. (Provision of agricultural machinery, fertilizers, seeds,breeding stock on favorable terms; land improvement; pest control; free agricultural advisory services and soil chemical analysis, etc.) In fulfilling these tasks, the professional organizations shall receive extensive state support. Above all, state intervention must enforce substantial reductions in the cost of artificial fertilizers and electrical power.

3. The corporative organizations also have the obligation to firmly integrate the occupational group of farmworkers into the agricultural professional community through socially equitable labor contracts. The state retains supervisory authority and supreme arbitration.

Capable farmworkers must be given the opportunity to advance to become settlers.

The necessary improvement in housing conditions and training for farmworkers will progress more rapidly and thoroughly as the overall situation of agriculture improves. Through these improvements for domestic farmworkers and by halting rural depopulation,the recruitment of foreign farmworkers becomes unnecessary and shall henceforth be prohibited.

4. The importance of the peasantry for the nation requires state and corporative support for vocational training and the revival of peasant culture. (Rural youth hostels, agricultural colleges with extensive benefits for impoverished but talented rural youth.)

5. Corporative economic organizations cannot provide decisive help to the peasantry—only the political significance of the NSDAP's freedom movement can.

The current distress of the rural population is part of the distress of the entire German people.

It is madness to believe that any single occupational group can detach itself from Germany's shared destiny, and a crime to pit rural against urban populations, who are inextricably bound together for better or worse.

Economic assistance within the framework of the prevailing political system cannot bring fundamental improvement; for the distress of the German people stems from its political constitution, which can only be overcome through political means.

The old political parties that have governed until now, which placed our people under this constitution, cannot lead the way to liberation.

Corporative organizations in our recent state have important economic tasks to fulfill and can already undertake preparatory work in this sense, but for the political struggle for liberation—which must first create the preconditions for a new economic order—they are unsuitable; for this struggle cannot be waged from the standpoint of any single occupational group but must be pursued from the standpoint of the entire nation.

Only a political freedom movement can successfully lead the struggle for liberation against our oppressors and their overseers—a movement that, while fully recognizing the importance of the rural population and agriculture for the nation as a whole, unites the nationally conscious members of all estates and strata of the German people.

This political freedom movement of the German people is the NSDAP.

signed, Adolf Hitler.